How to Paint Watercolour

Prosenjit Saha & Arundhati Saha

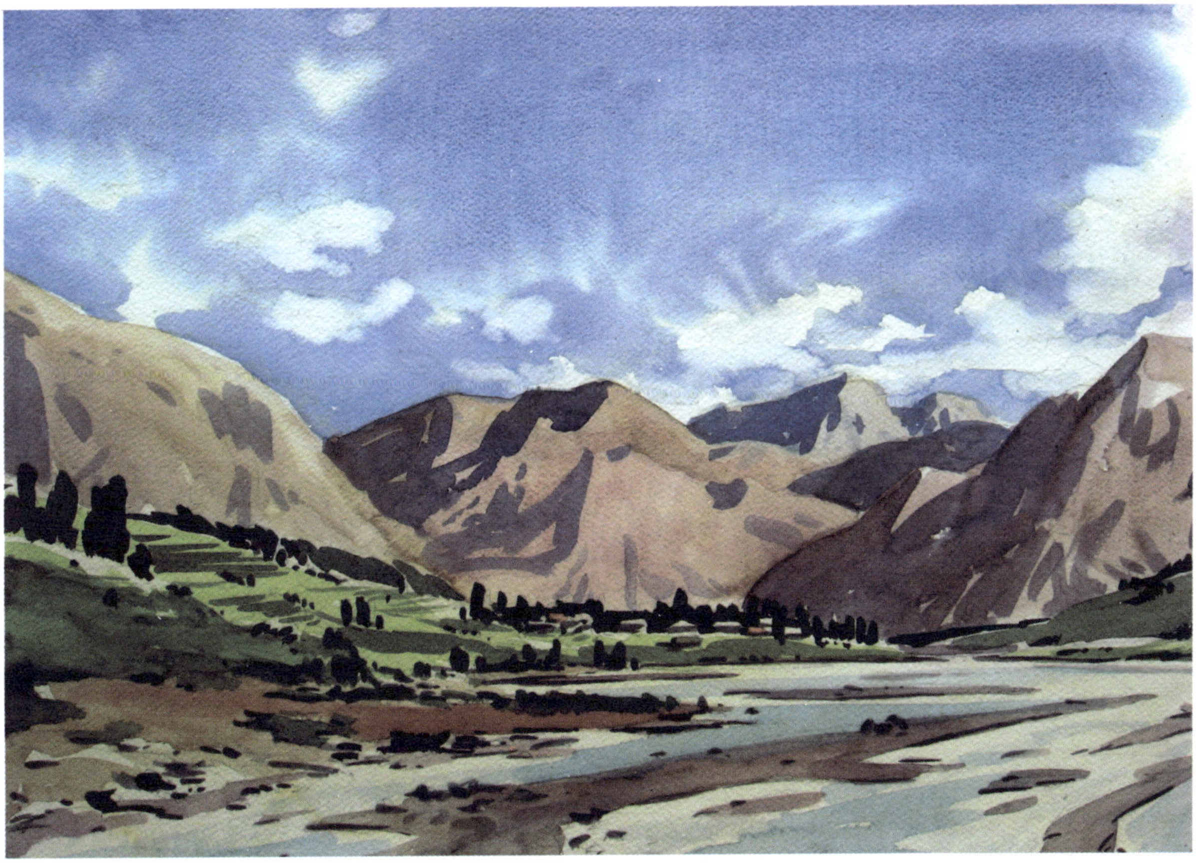

AF658581

UNICORN
ART BOOKS

Publishers
UNICORN BOOKS

F-2/16, Ansari Road, Daryaganj, New Delhi-110002

E-mail: info@unicornbooks.in • *Website:* www.unicornbooks.in

☎ 011-23275434, 23262683

Branch : Mumbai

23-25, Zaoba Wadi Thakurdwar, Mumbai-401002

☎ 022-22010941, 022-22053387

E-mail: rapidex@bom5.vsnl.net.in

ISBN: 978-81-7806-300-3

(How to Paint Watercolour)

Edition: 2016

Printed at : Param Offsetters, Okhla, New Delhi-110020

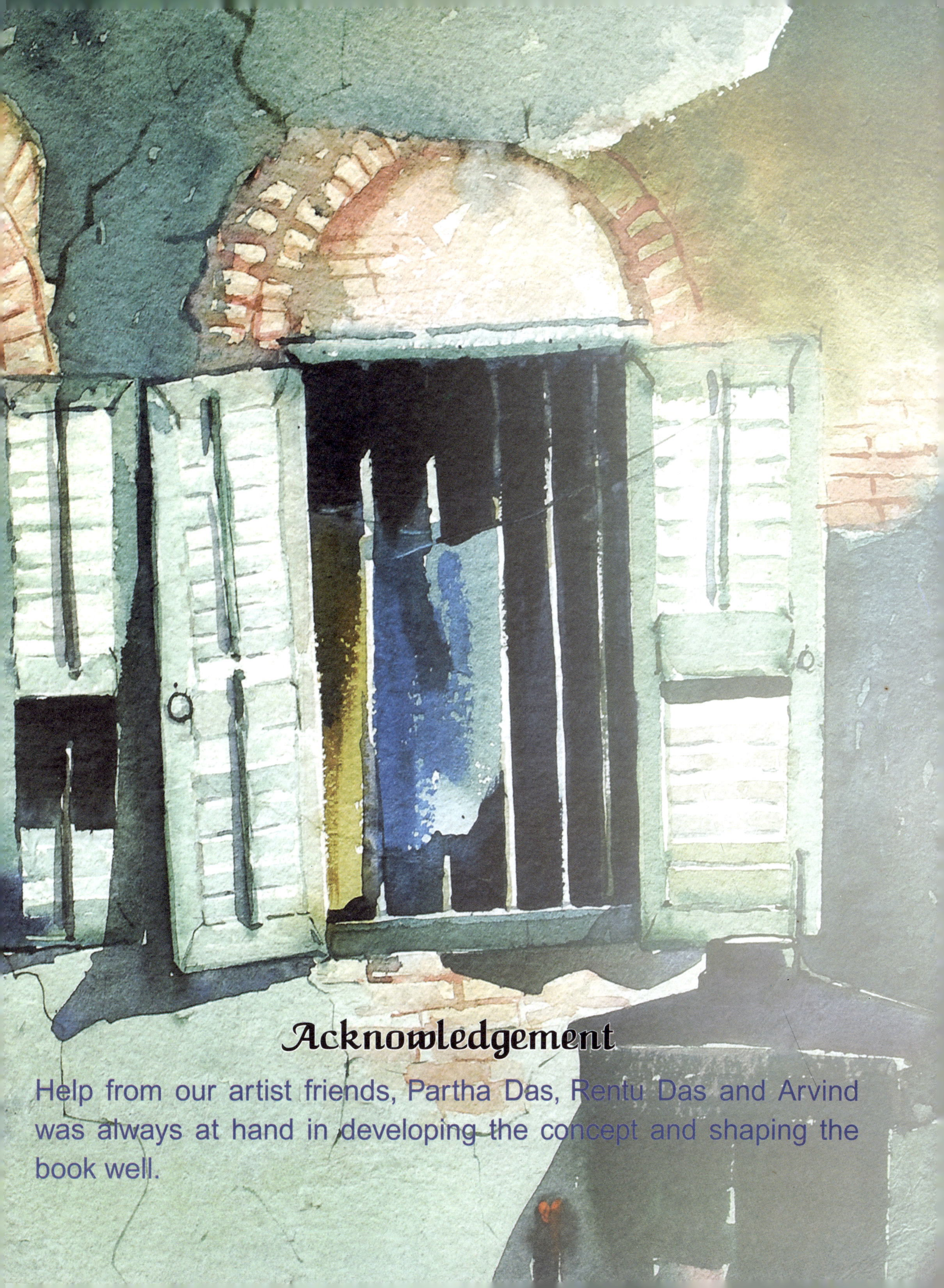

Acknowledgement

Help from our artist friends, Partha Das, Rentu Das and Arvind was always at hand in developing the concept and shaping the book well.

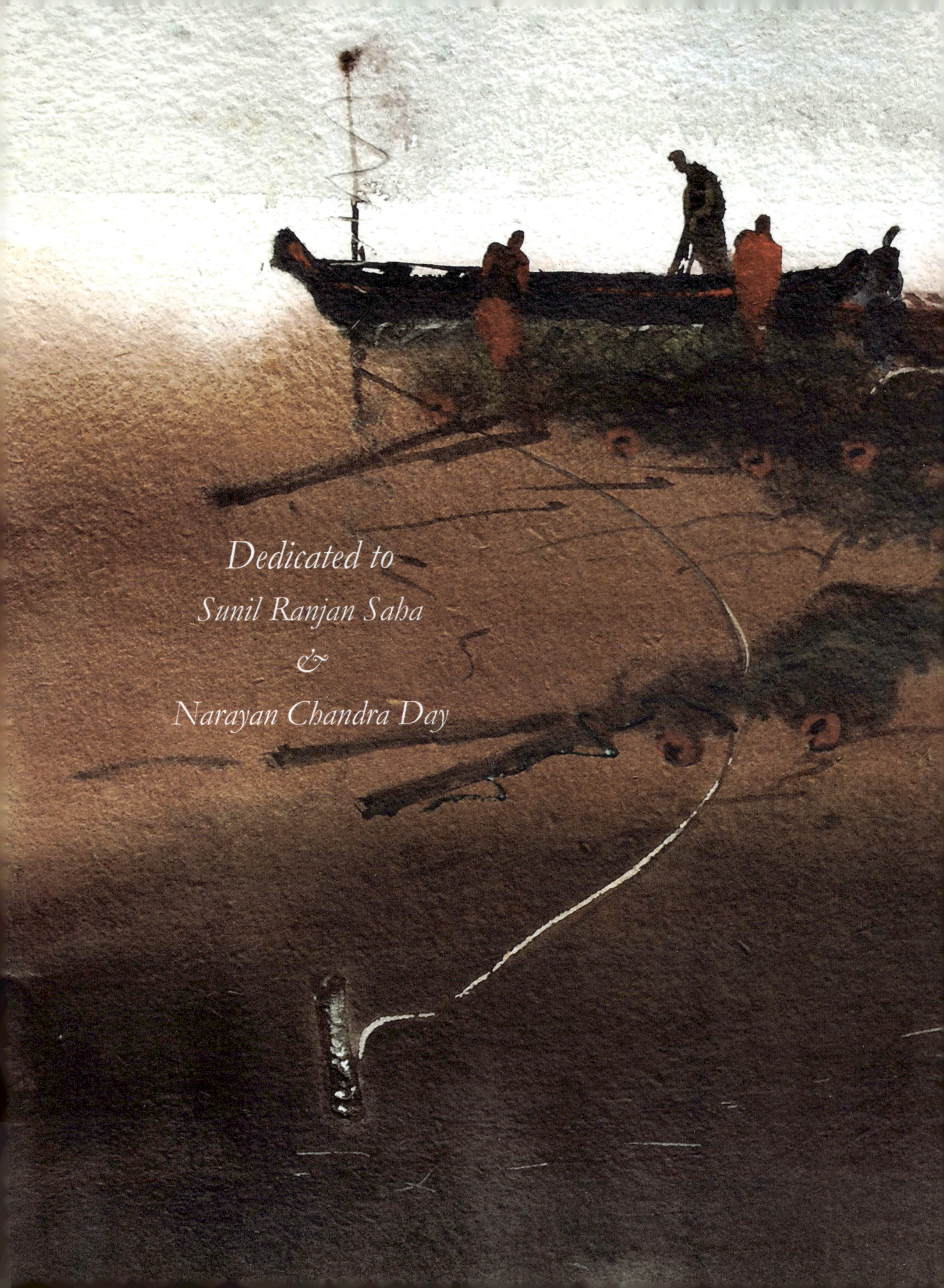

Dedicated to

Sunil Ranjan Saha

&

Narayan Chandra Day

Contents

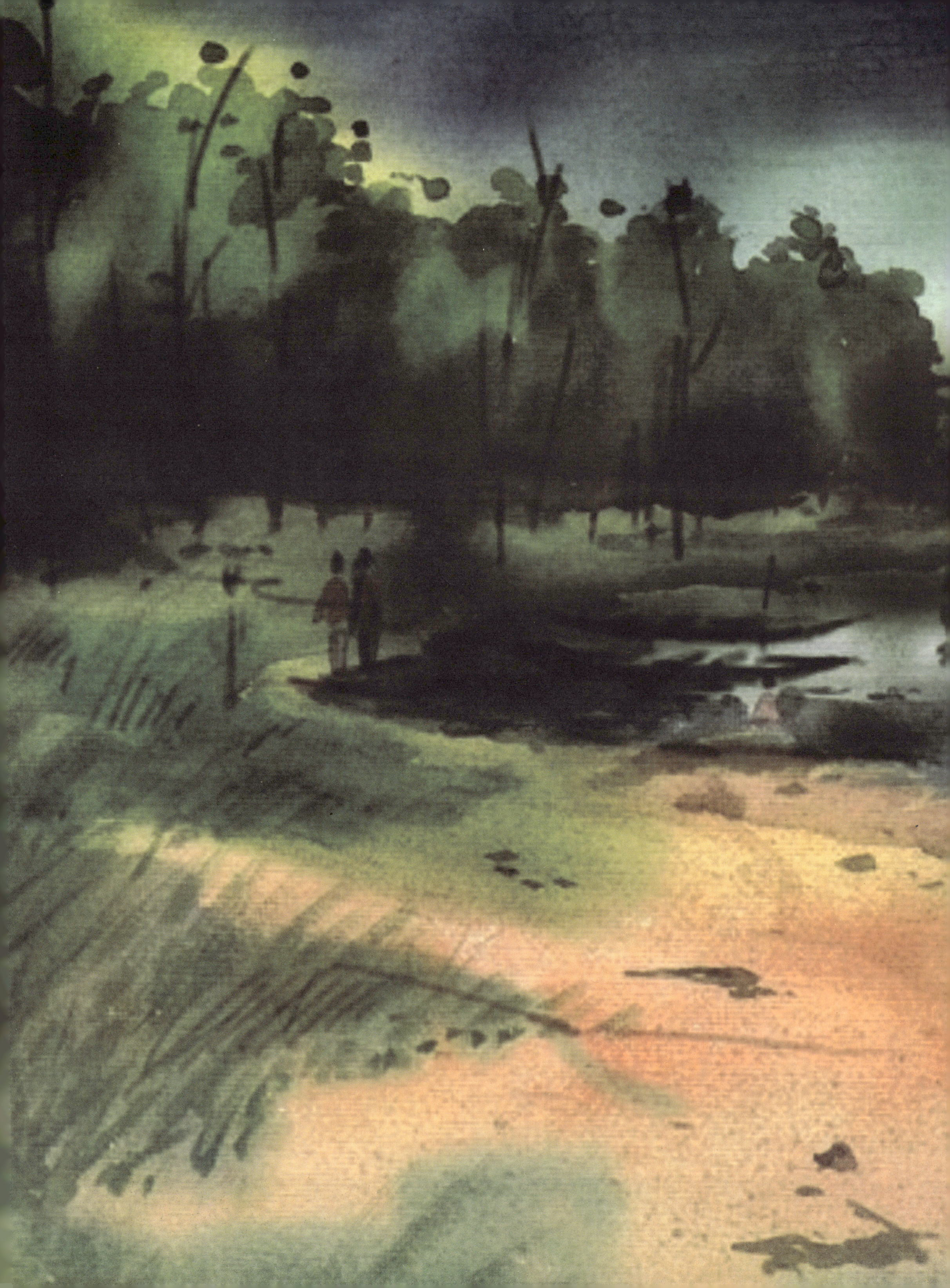

History of Watercolour

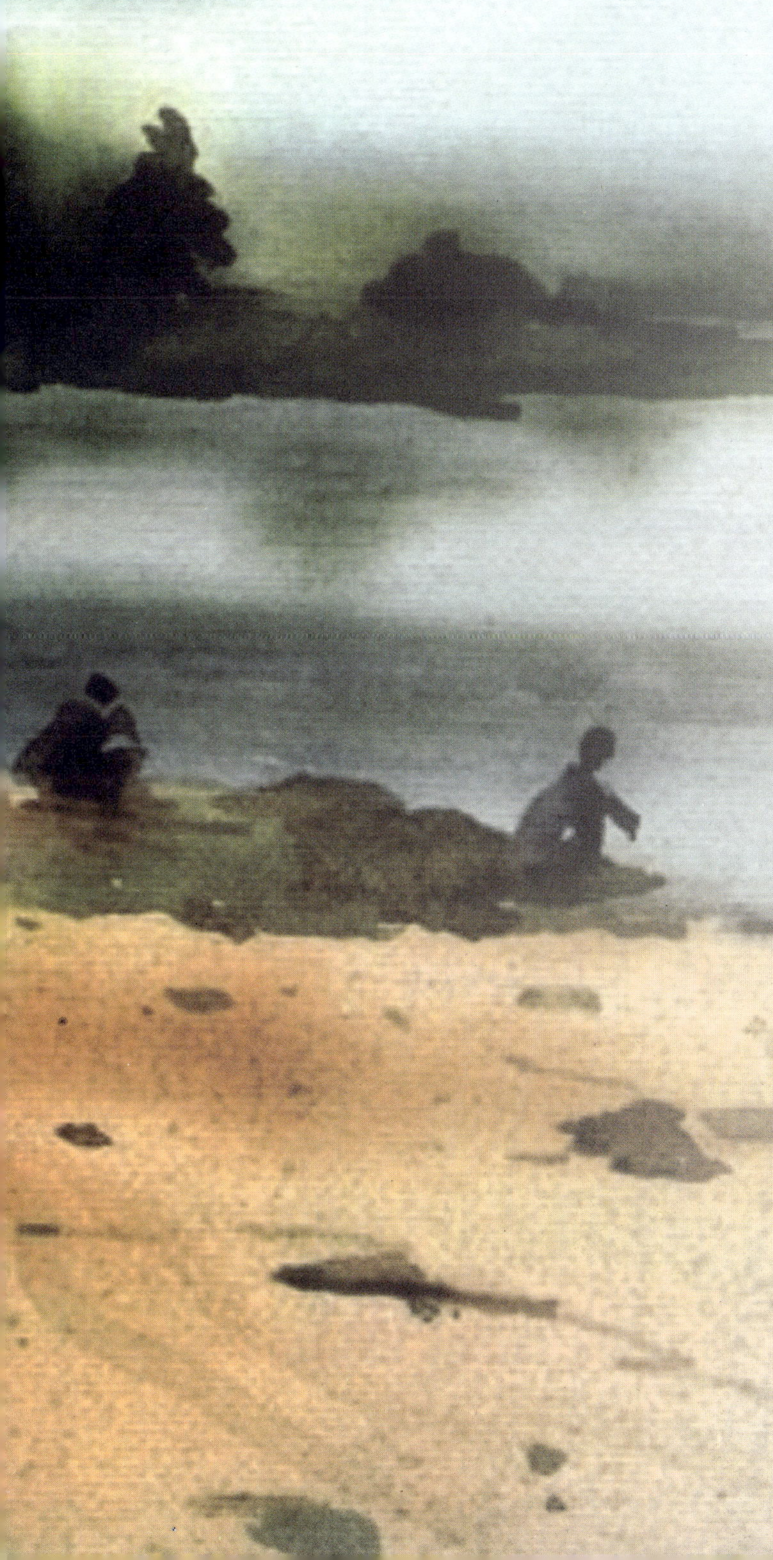

Watercolour is a painting method in which a type of paint composed of water-soluble dried pigments is used. Painting by watercolours is like shooting an arrow that, once shot, cannot be undone and the original one cannot be retrieved. If you put colour over a previous work, the two shall mix, producing a different and unexpected colour and in the process even the paper surface may get damaged.

Two British painters of the eighteenth century, Joseph Turner and John Constable brought in vogue the watercolour as an independent genre. Thereafter, John Singer Sargent, Winslow Homer and William Russell Flint took this art to new heights.

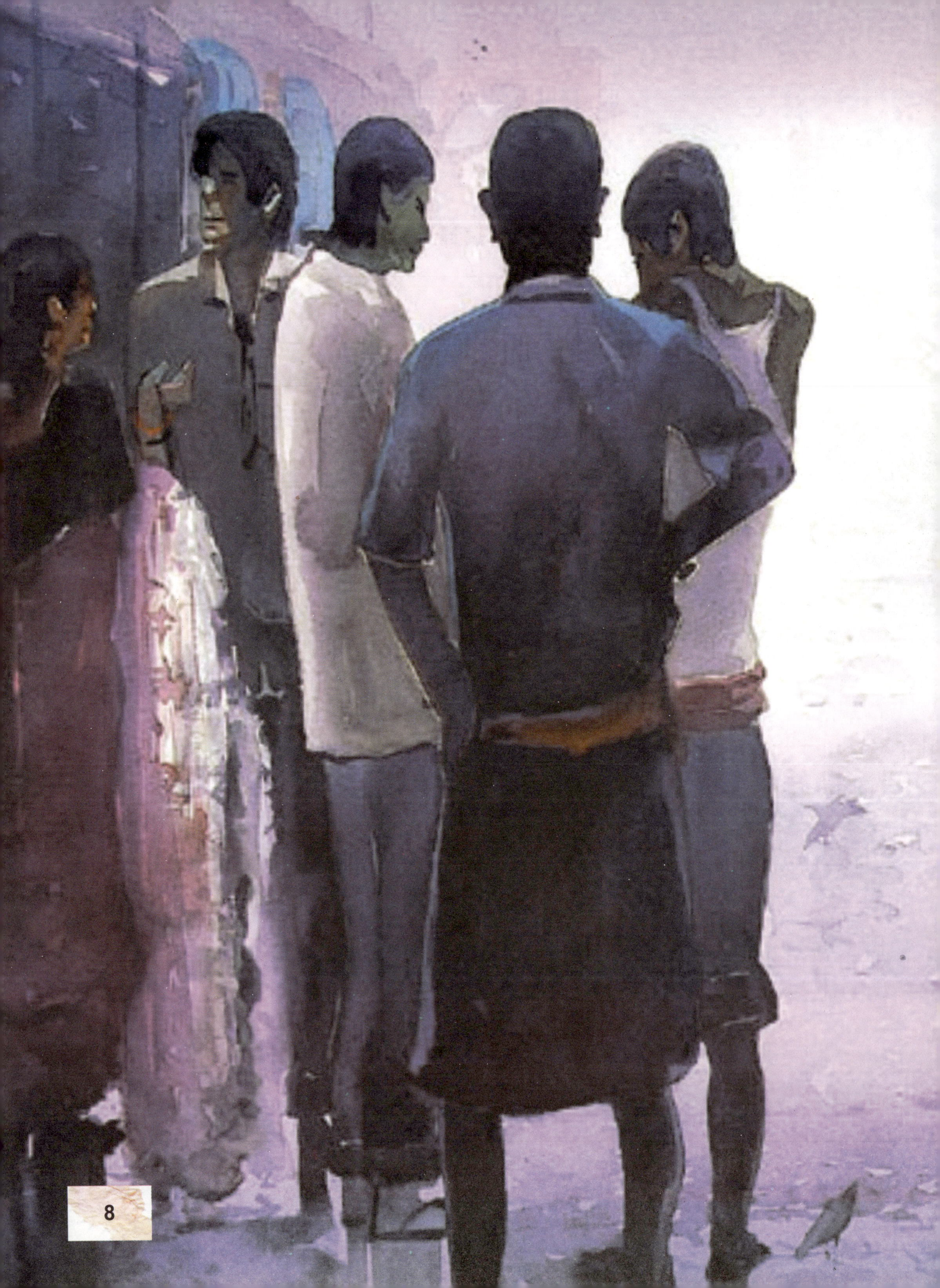

Introduction

Nature provides almost everything to us. All elements that we require can be found in the nature.

To study this book we must be familiar with line drawing, perspective, pencil shading and colour. While studying this book we will combine the light source and the perspective of the subject. It also helps us to understand the character of individual subjects like tree, water, mountain, human figure, etc. We also study about compositions and how to select outdoor and indoor compositions.

While reading 'Let's Paint Watercolour' do keep all these above mentioned points in your mind and go through this book readily as it will aid you to understand the basics of drawing and colour as well as other related aspects properly.

We assure you that you will be able to grasp and see a big change in your artistic talents by the time you reach the last page.

❑❑❑

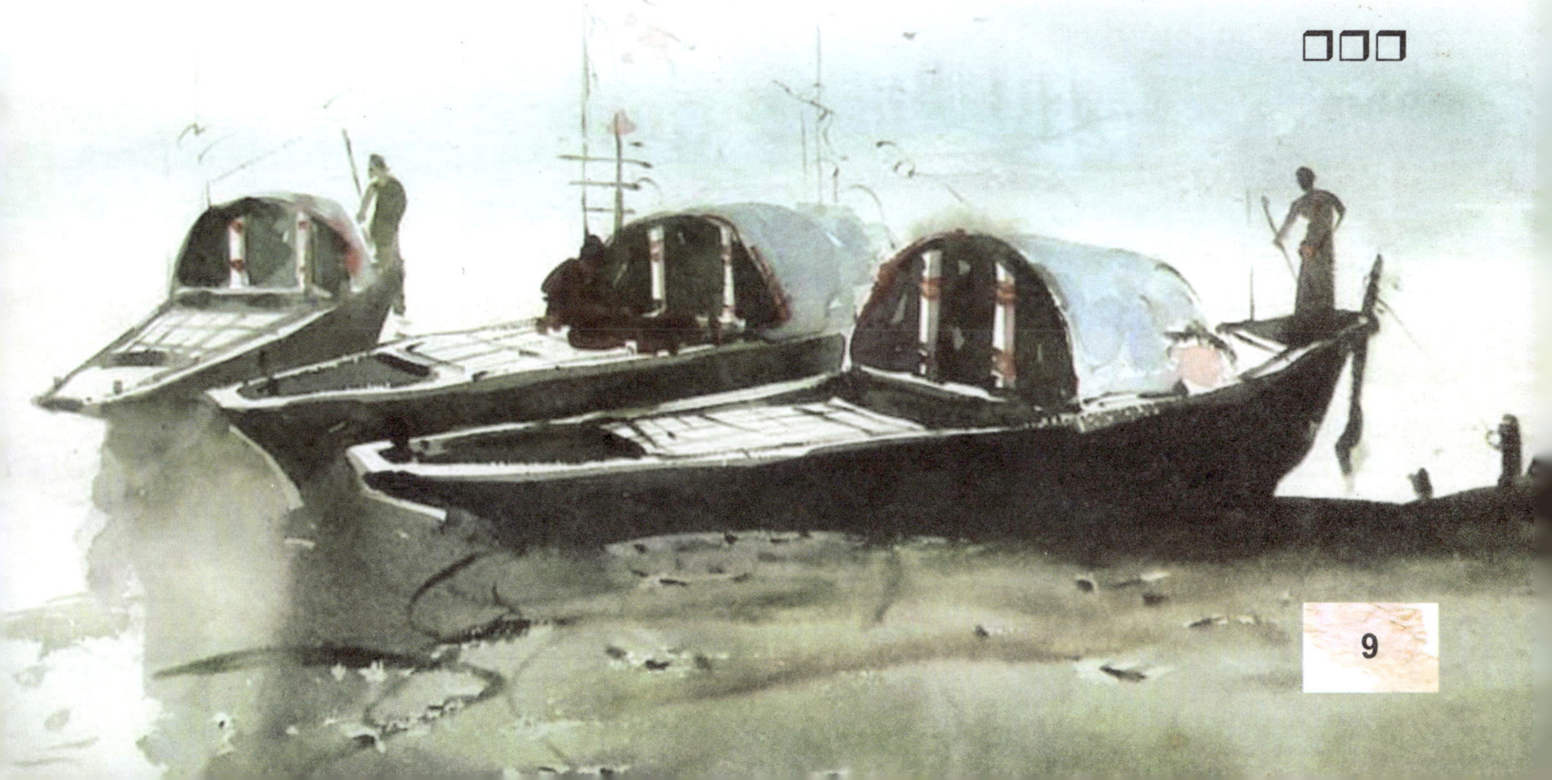

Materials

Palettes

A palette is designed to make available many paints at one time and to mix them as required. Generally, palettes come with small depressions made for various paints along the edges (two rows) and half a dozen larger depressions for colour-mixing. There is no hard-and-fast rule, but normally warm colours are squeezed out in one row and cool ones in the other.

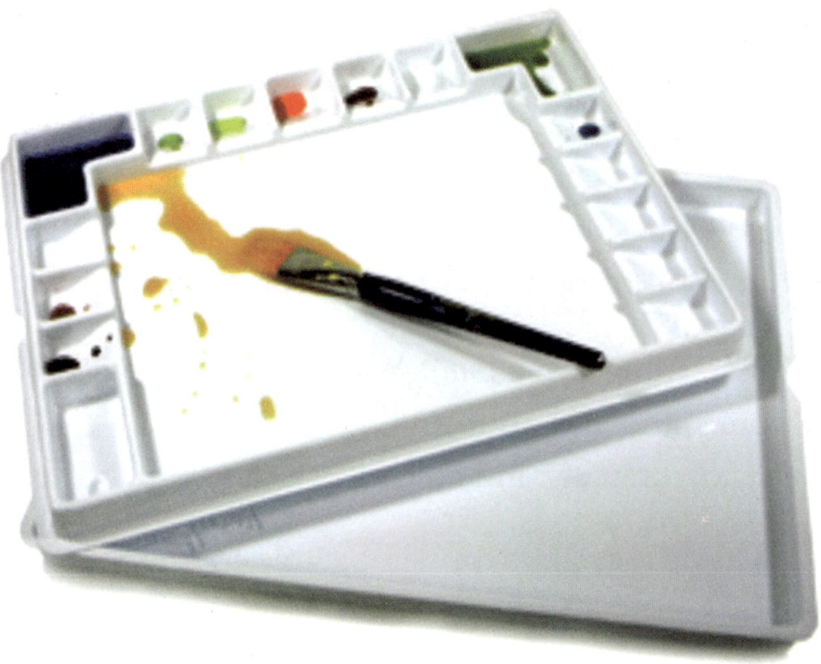

Colours

Today we have a wide variety of transparent colours at our disposal, which can be mixed as per our requirements to carry desired shades in our paintings. Out of the vast range of shades that are available, it is wise to stick to a limited palette and gain mastery over it.

Colours are available in the form of solid (cakes) or semi-solid pigments (tubes).

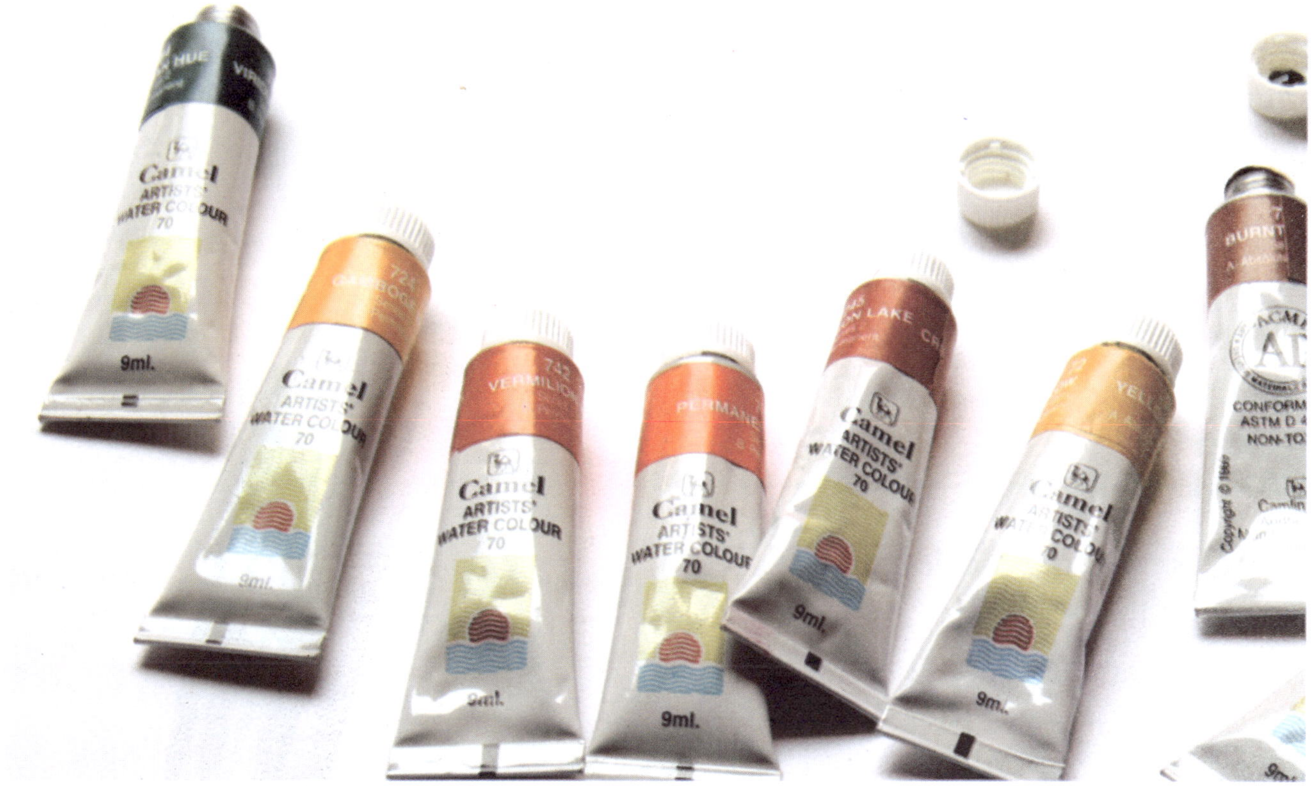

TUBES

In tubes, colours are readily available in a semi-liquid paste which can be squeezed out on the palette for further mixing with water in desired proportions.

CAKES

Some colours come in solid cakes in a box, and are to be used by applying a wet brush to them.

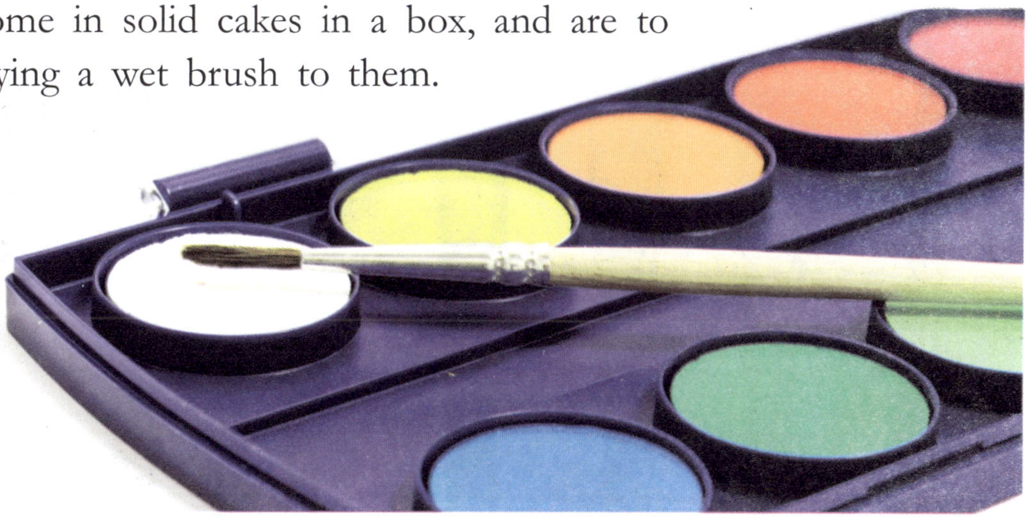

Since this process yields colours in a small quantity, cakes are unsuitable for works that require large washes. Therefore, their use is limited.

Out of the vast range of shades that are available, it is wise to stick to a limited palette and gain mastery over it.

Brushes

They come in mainly three types:

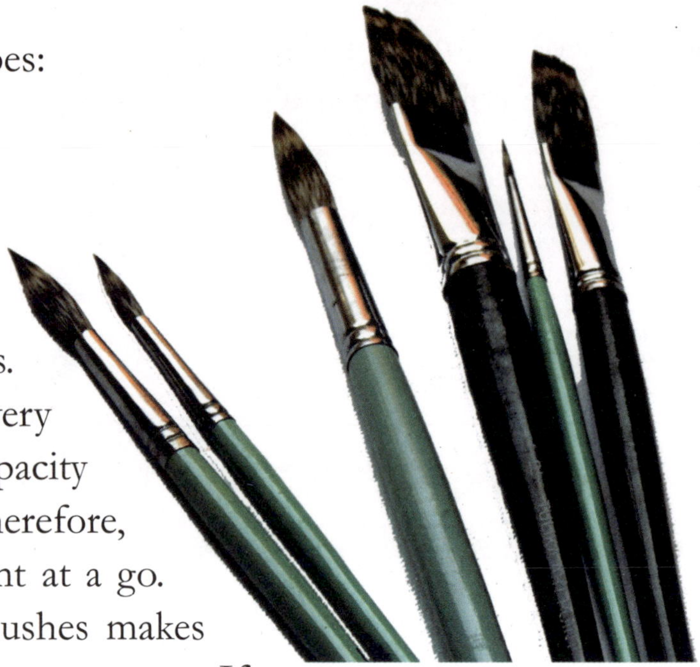

SABLE HAIR BRUSH

Sable is a brown-coloured animal whose hair is used for making these brushes. Sable hair brushes have a very soft texture and excellent capacity of holding wet paint. It is, therefore, easy to pick a lot of wet paint at a go. The soft texture of these brushes makes putting down washes on paper very easy. If used carefully, these brushes can last a lifetime. Being excellent in quality, these brushes are naturally expensive.

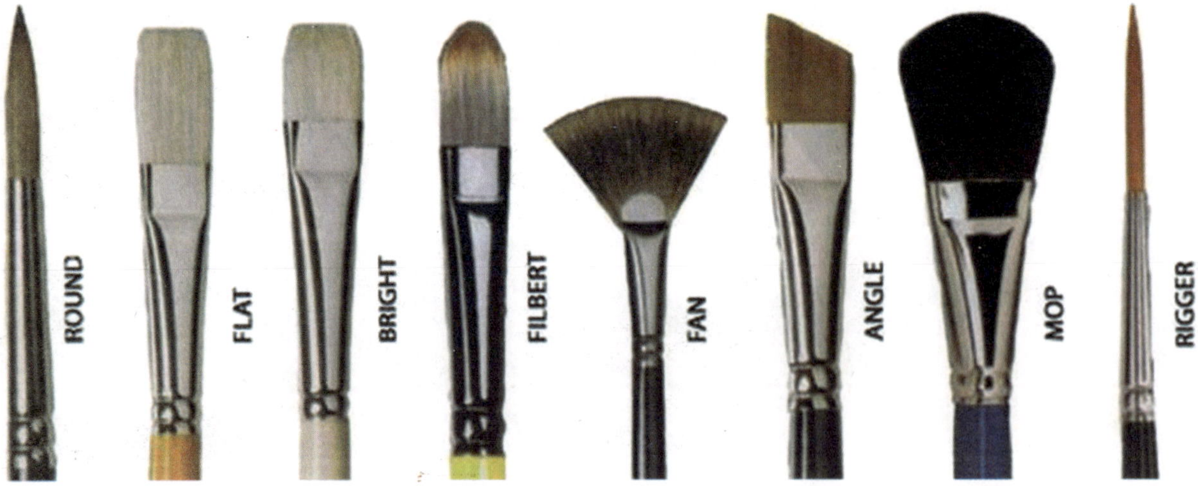

SQUIRREL HAIR BRUSH

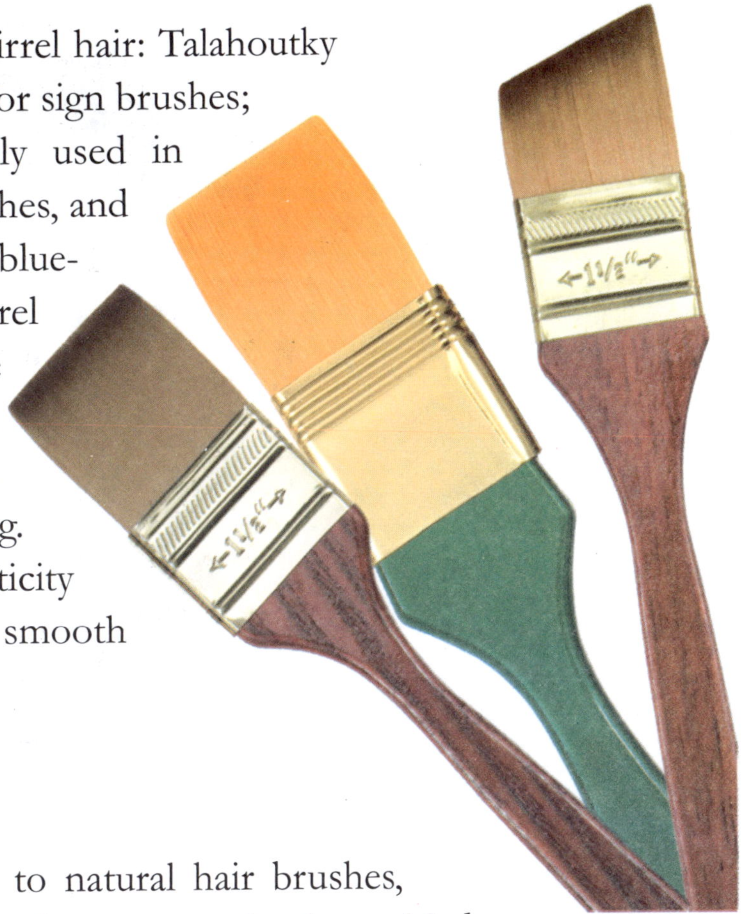

There are three main types of Squirrel hair: Talahoutky is brown in color and used mainly for sign brushes; Kazan is brown-black and mainly used in brushes for watercolour, wash brushes, and watercolour mops; Sacamena is blue-black, the softest of all the Squirrel hair, and is used for making some of the best watercolour brushes. This soft, absorbent hair points well when wet, but has little spring. Squirrel hair brush has good elasticity and are ideal for washes, letting and smooth painted finishes.

SYNTHETIC HAIR BRUSH

A good & economical alternative to natural hair brushes, these are available in a wide variety of textures and colours. Made using polyester filaments of different thickness, synthetic hair now offers almost all properties of natural hair including colour retention, spring-back, strength and fine tips.

Shapes

The styles of brush tip seen most commonly are:

- **Round:** pointed tip, long closely arranged bristles for detail
- **Flat:** mainly to apply large washes and also to draw clear and sharp edges wherever desired. Available in widths ranging from quarter-inch to two inches, and even more. For spreading paint quickly and evenly over a surface. They will have longer hairs than their Bright counterpart.

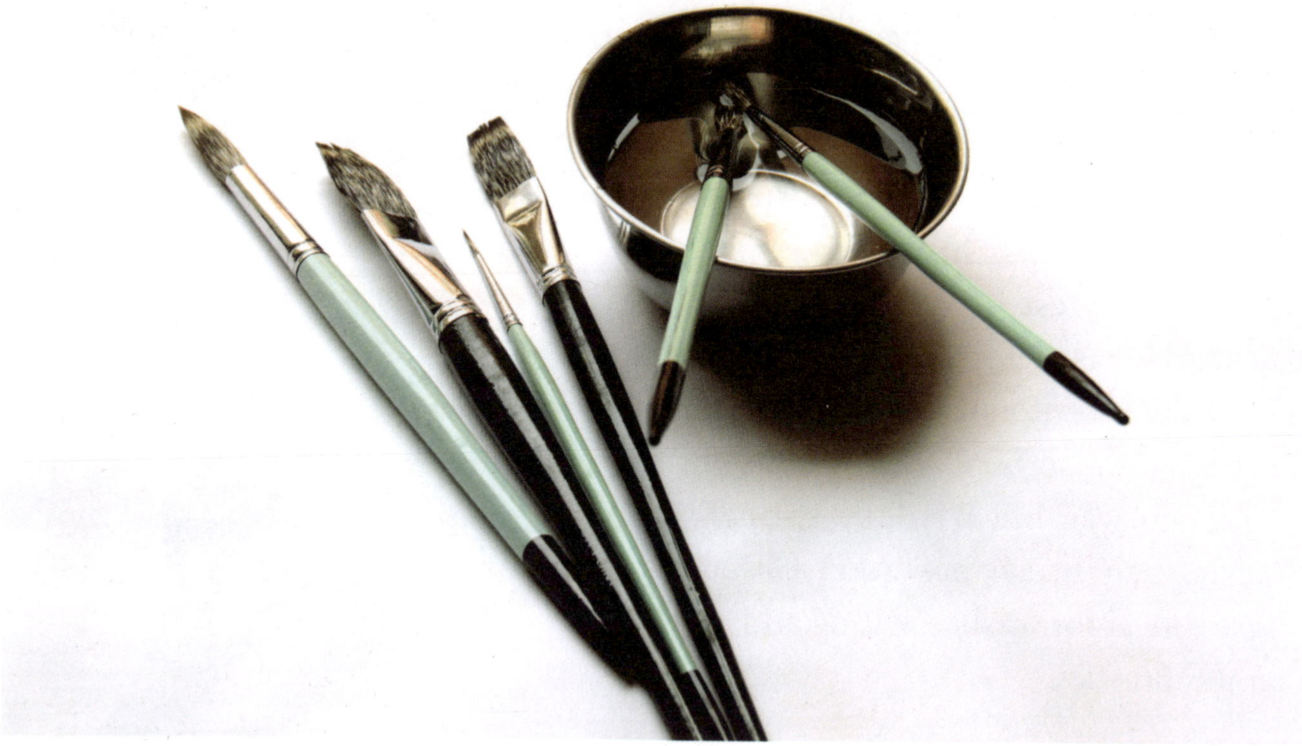

- **Bright:** shorter than flats. Flat brushes with short stiff bristles, good for driving paint into the weave of a canvas in thinner paint applications, as well as thicker painting styles

- **Filbert:** flat brushes with domed ends. They allow good coverage and the ability to perform some detail work.

- **Fan:** for blending broad areas of paint.

- **Angle:** like the filbert, these are versatile and can be applied in both general painting application as well as some detail work.

- **Mop:** a larger format brush with a rounded edge for broad soft paint application as well as for getting thinner glazes over existing drying layers of paint without damaging lower layers.

- **Rigger:** round brushes with longish hairs, traditionally used for painting the rigging in pictures of ships. They are useful for fine lines and are versatile for both oils and watercolours.

Paper

Among the materials used for watercolours, paper is perhaps the most important as the final results of a painting change with the paper quality. Good quality white paper is the most suitable for transparent watercolours. For Gouache, acrylic and such other opaque mediums, brown paper, box-board or tinted paper can be used.

Papers are also divided into Handmade and Machine-made.

Handmade paper is the most suitable paper for watercolours.

Depending upon the surface quality, it is classified into Smooth, Rough and Matte. Each surface texture has a distinct effect on the paints used.

Imported papers are also available nowadays. These are hot-pressed (smoother) or cold-pressed (rougher) – the latter being more suitable for watercolours.

❑❑❑

Colour Wheel

The colour wheel is a simple device to understand colours in relation to each other.

The various classifications such as secondary colours can be obtained by mixing primary colours. Complementary colours as well as warm/cool colours can be appreciated by just a glance at the Colour Wheel.

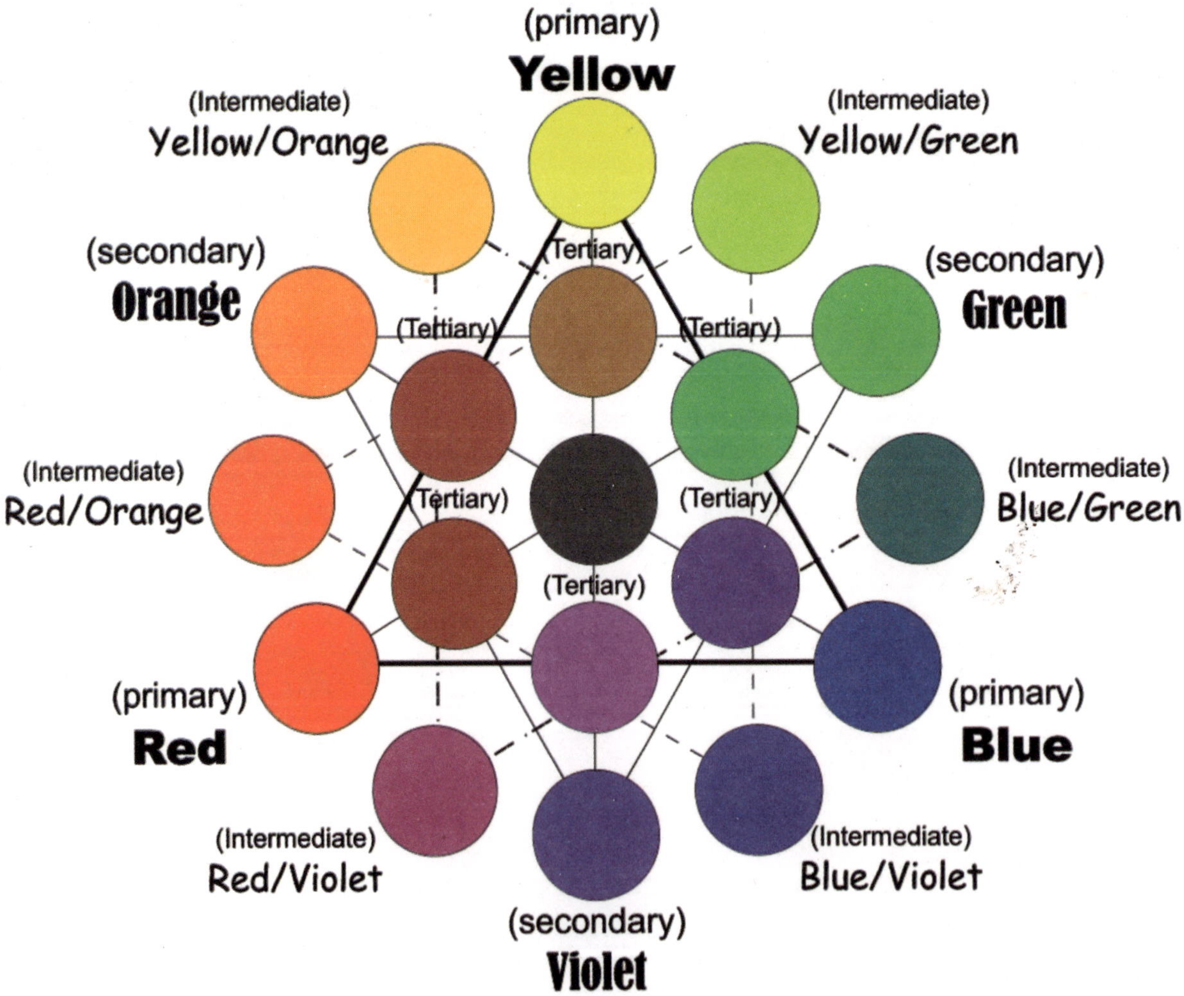

Warm/Cool Colours

Colours are classified as warm and cool colours. Red, Yellow, Orange and Brown are warm colours. These colours excite the mind. Blue, Green, Violet on the other hand are cool colours. These colours soothe the mind. This classification of colours, obviously, is based on the effect they have on the viewer's mind.

Of the two, warm colours are aggressive – they make their effect felt first; and the cool colours later. Even in the painting, the plane of the warm colours appears to be in the foreground, while the cool colours are relegated to the background. Therefore, to create the effect of depth of distance in the painting, the foregrounds should be painted in warm colours and cool colours should be used for the portions that are in the rear/distance.

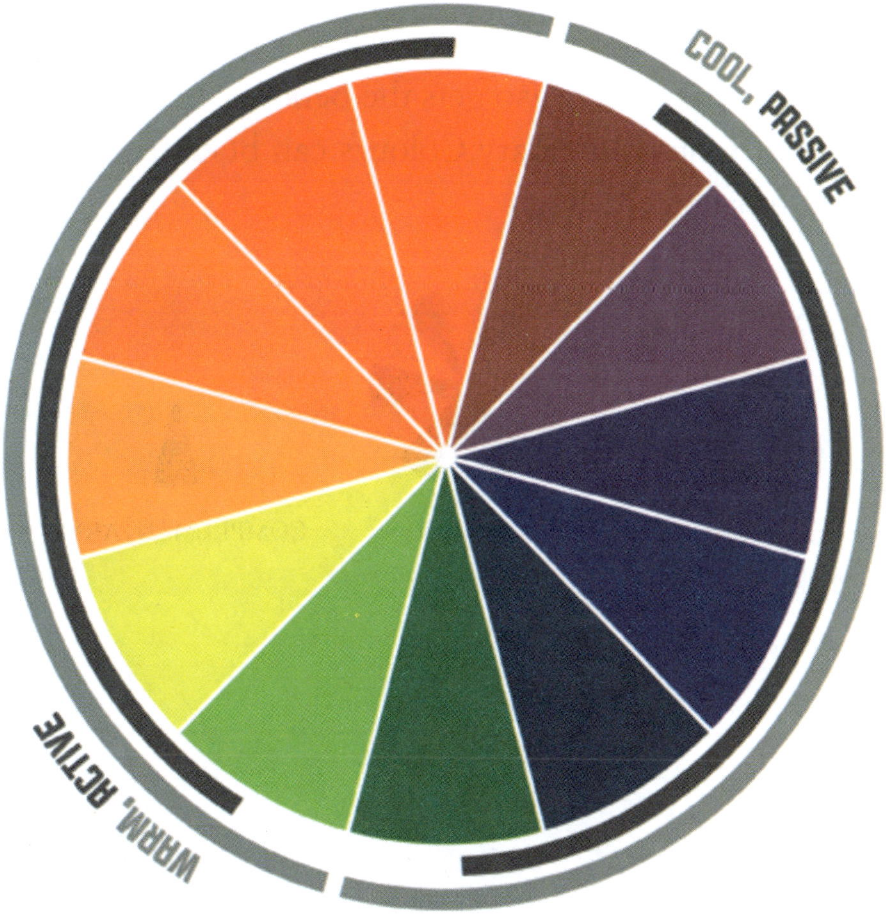

PRIMARY COLOURS

Red, Blue and Yellow are Primary Colours, they are also called 'Basic Colours' as all other colours are obtained by mixing them.

SECONDARY COLOURS

By mixing Red and Blue, we get Violet. Blue and Yellow gives us Green, whereas Yellow and Red gives us Orange. Thus the colours obtained from the mixture of Primary Colours are called Secondary Colours.

COMPLEMENTARY COLOURS

These are the colours appearing opposite each other in the colour wheel. Thus, for instance, Red and Green are complementary to each other. Yellow-Violet is another such pair. It is very important to understand this, because when painted side by side, complementary colours produce a striking visual effect: If Red is applied next to Green, the Green also gets the benefit of the company of the Red. This characteristic of Complementary Colours can be used to great advantage to make our painting more interesting.

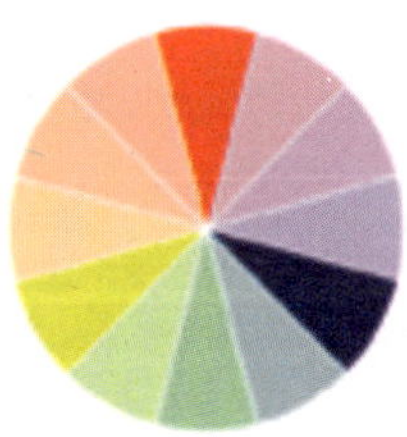

PRIMARY

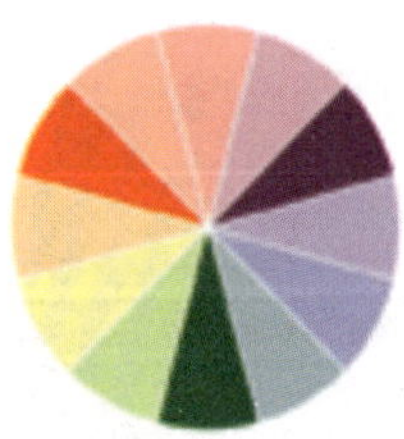

SECONDARY

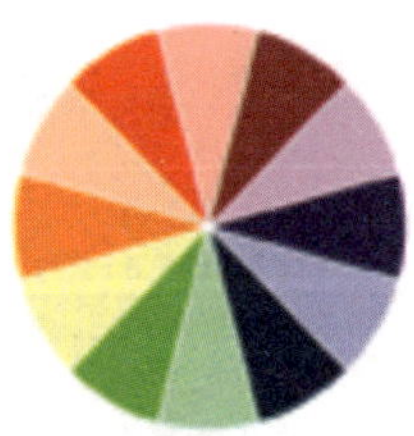

TERTIARY

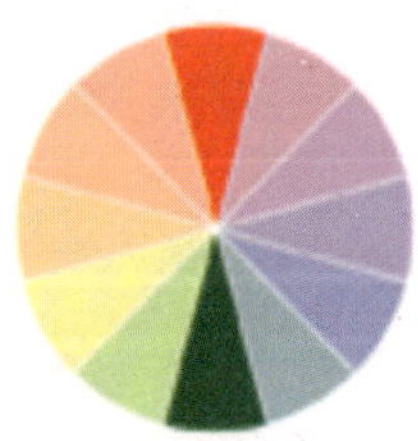

COMPLEMENTARY

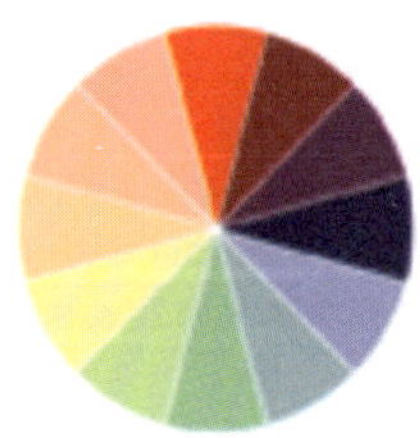

ANALOGOUS

Perspective

Any object that we see has three dimensions: length, breadth and depth. However, the picture which we are to paint on the paper has only length and breadth. The technique to create the illusion of depth (the third dimension) on the two-dimensional paper is called Perspective.

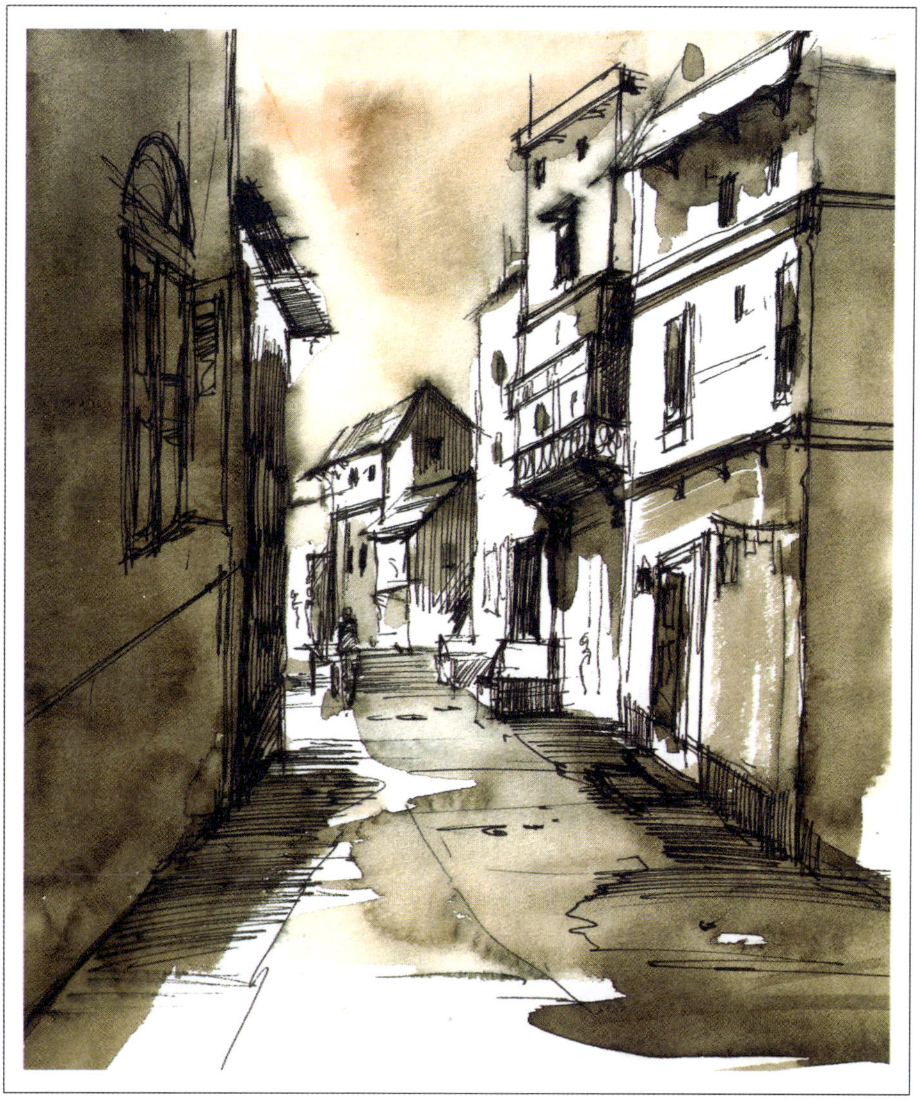

One-Point Perspective

One-point perspective relies on the premise that all parallel receding lines converge at one point along a horizon line. Lines that do not recede will be drawn as either horizontal or vertical lines.

HORIZON LINE

Your horizon line is always at eye-level. For example: if you are 6'4" tall, your horizon line (eye-level) will probably be 6 feet off the ground (assuming a measurement of 4" from the top of your head down to your eyes).

To find your horizon line in any room walk right up to the wall you want to draw - your horizon line will be on the same level as your eyes. You can even put a piece of tape at eye-level to remind you as you draw.

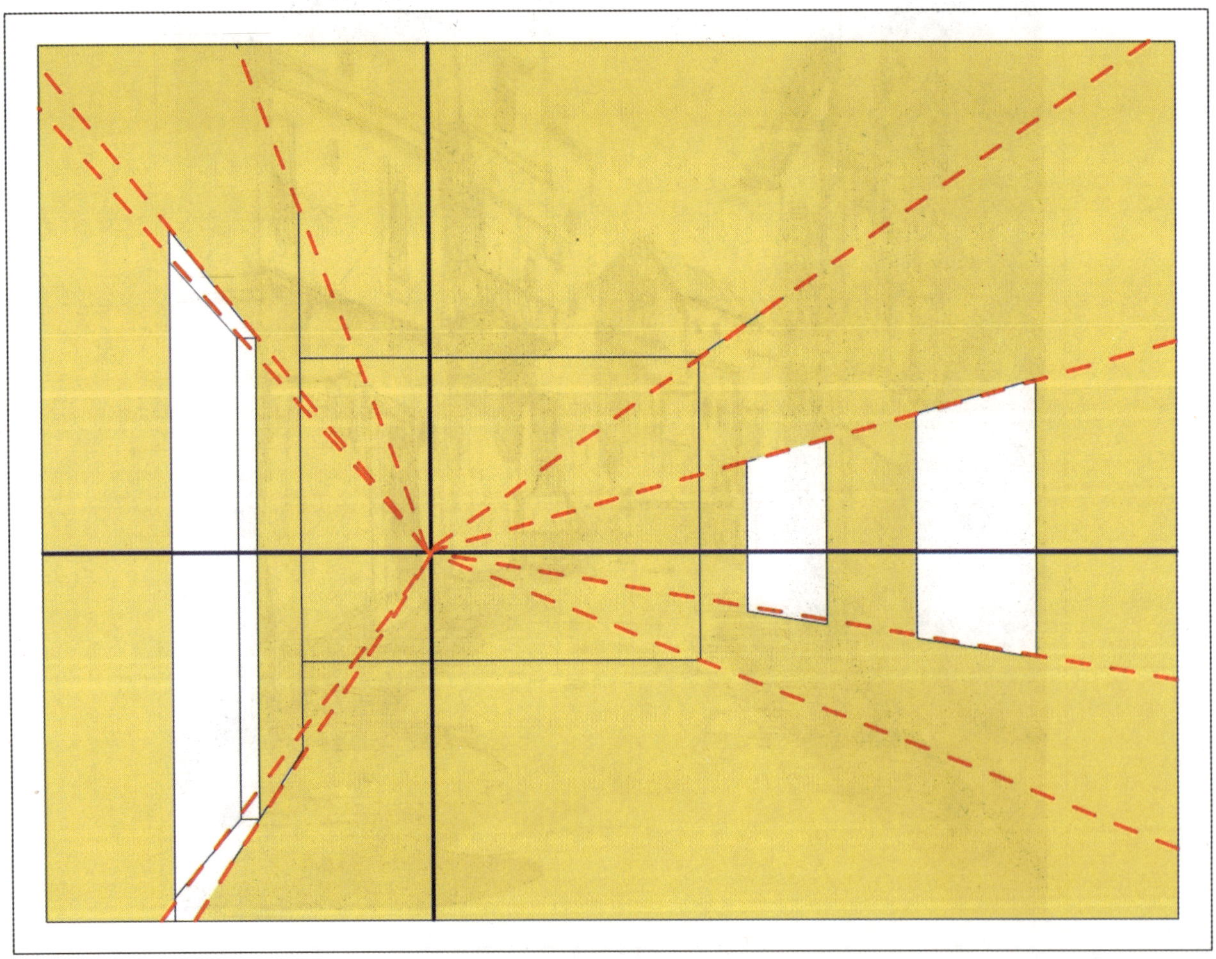

VANISHING POINT

The vanishing point must be on the horizon line. If you are looking down a hallway, your vanishing point will be directly in front of you, at a point right between your eyes.

Two-Point Perspective

Two-point perspective relies on the premise that all receding lines converge at one of two points along the horizon line. Lines that do not recede will be drawn only as vertical lines.

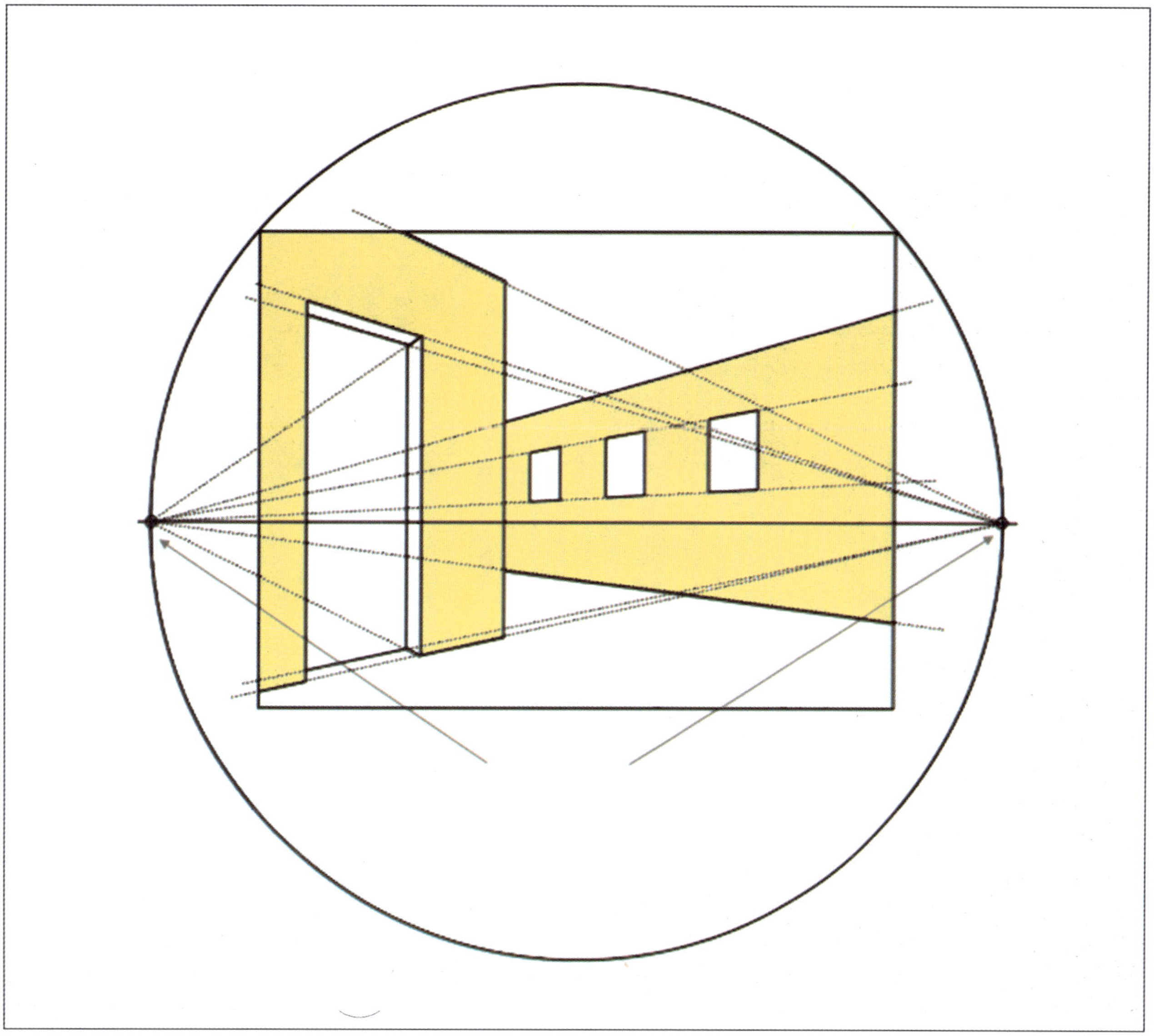

HORIZON LINE

In both one and two point perspective, your horizon line will always be the same as your eye level. For example, if you are resting your chin on the floor your eye level will be about 4 inches off the ground (assuming a measurement of 4 inches from chin to eyes).

VANISHING POINTS

Both vanishing points must lie on the horizon line. Receding lines from the wall to your right will converge at a vanishing point to the left while the receding lines from the wall to your left will converge at a point to the right. The location of each vanishing point (how far left or right) will depend on your viewpoint (the angle at which you view the corner of a room or object).

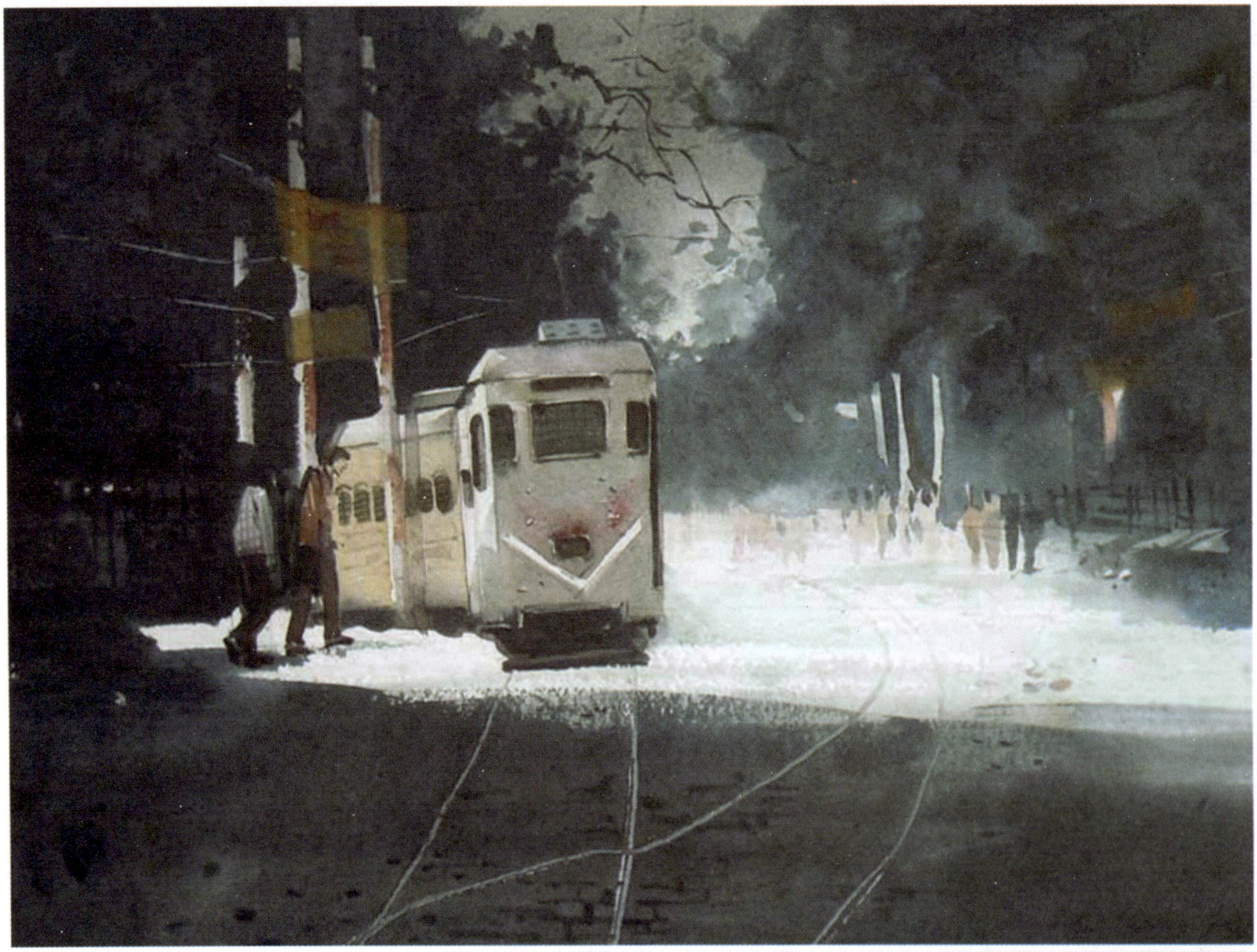

Some Examples of Perspective Drawing

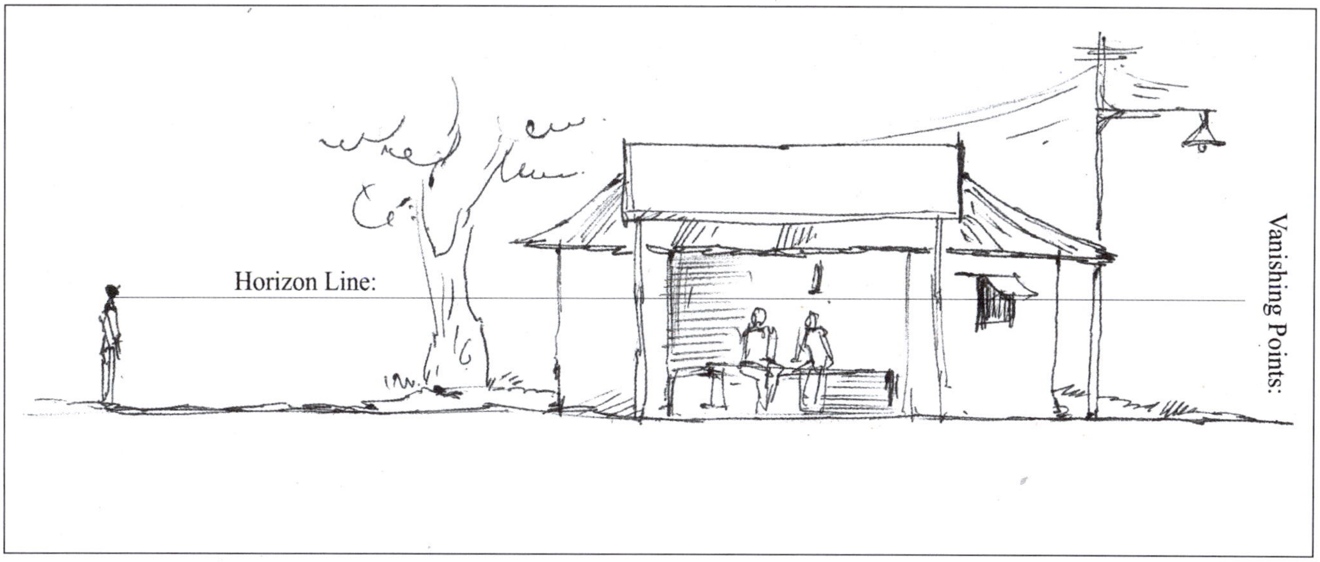

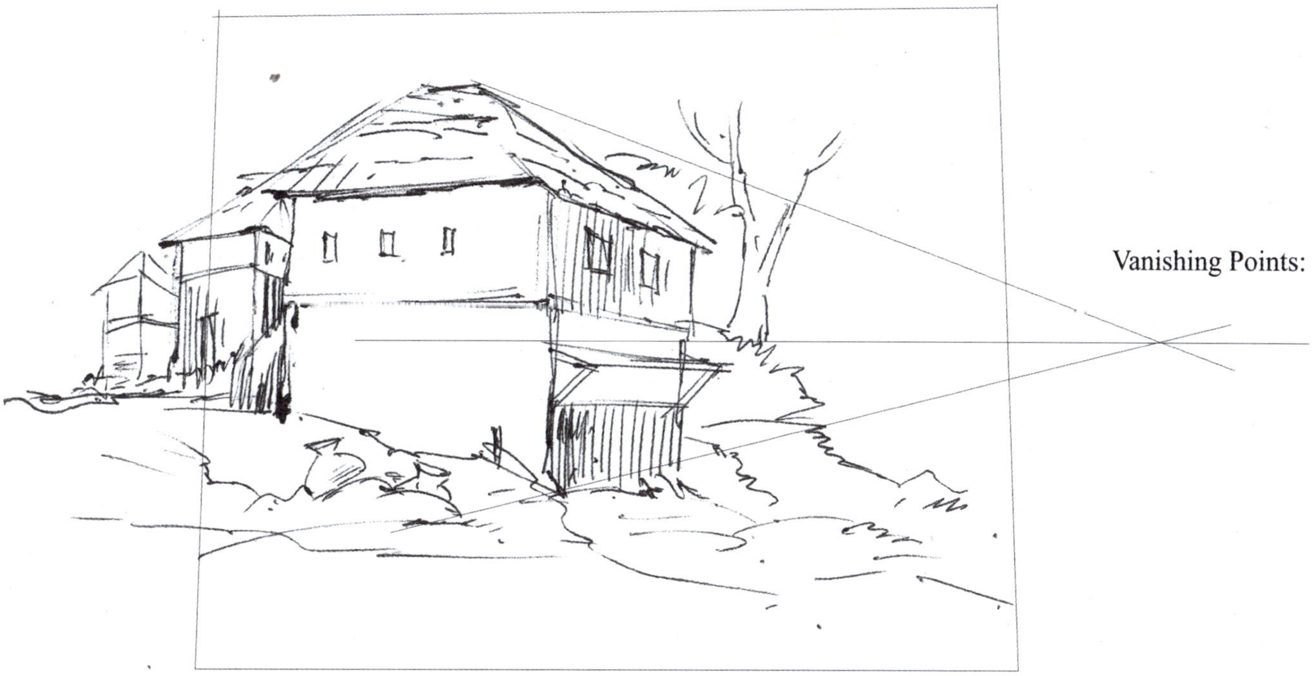

❒❒❒

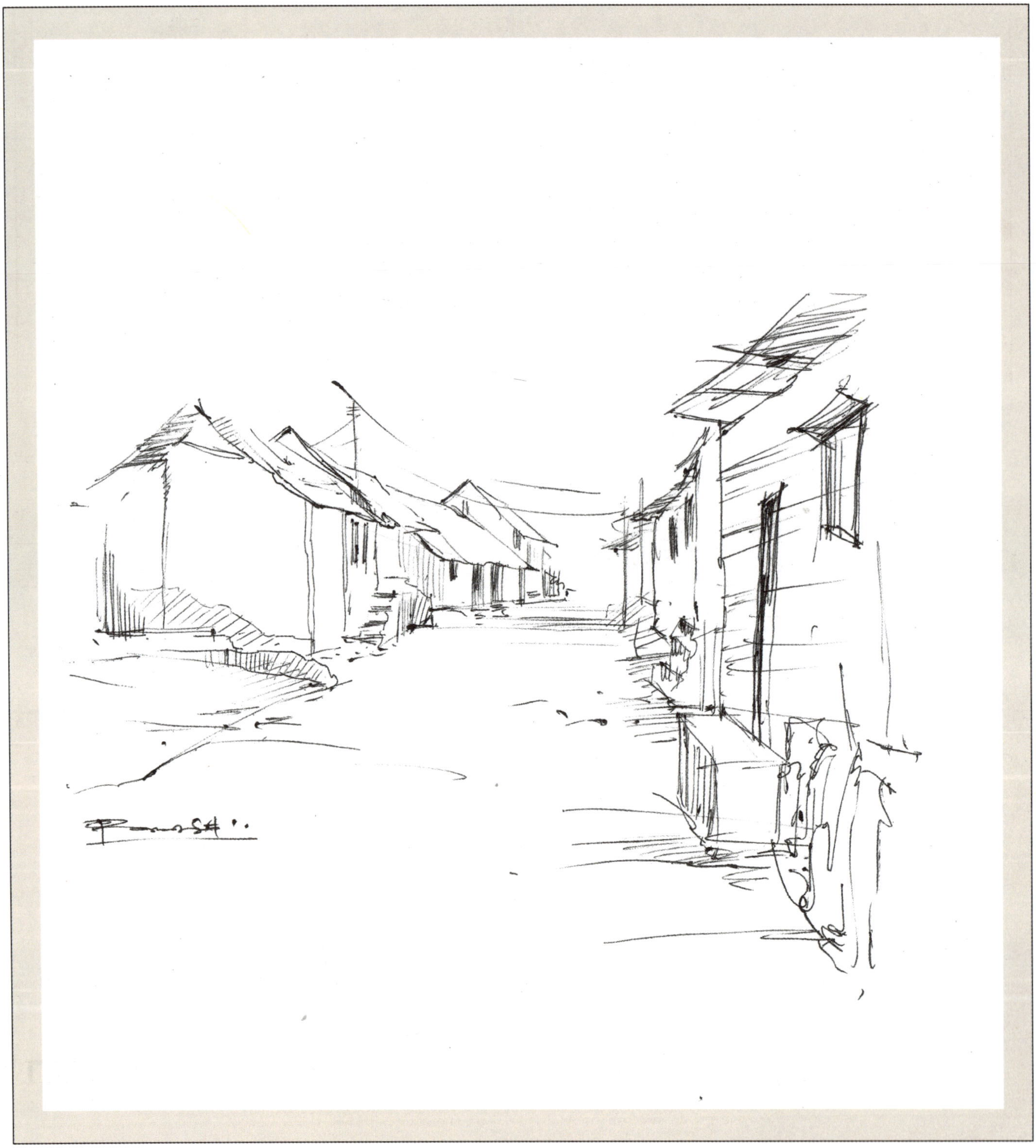

Sketching

Drawing is the basis of painting and the beginning of drawing is sketching. Once this foundation is laid, one can readily build on it, whether the painting is Realistic or Abstract.

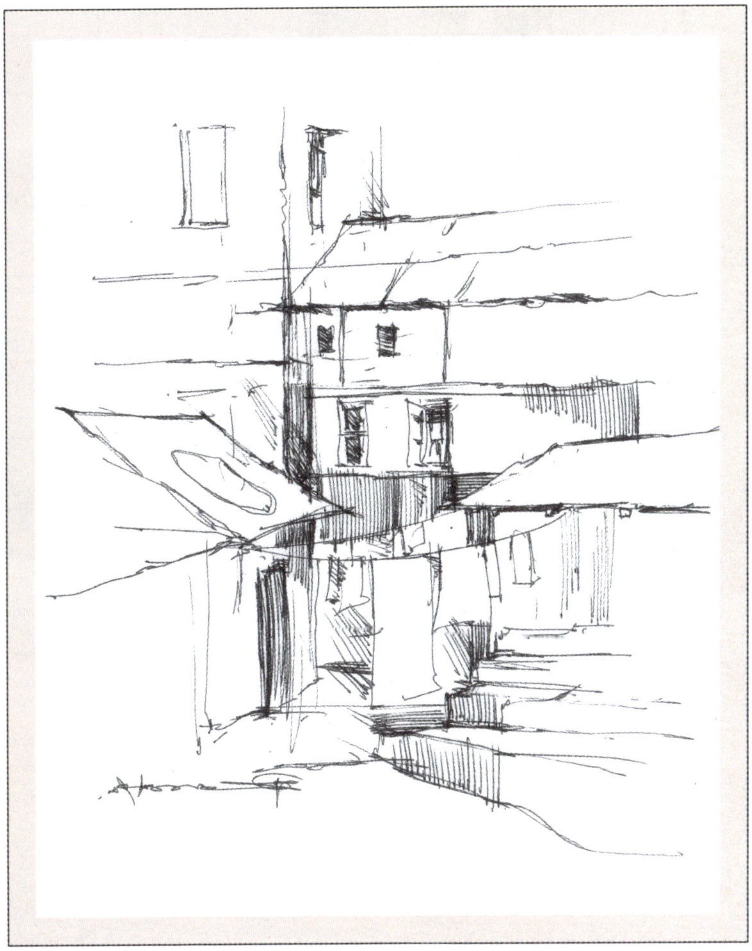

There are a number of reasons for undertaking sketching:

- It helps to loosen-up our hands.
- It helps to retain ideas or concepts for future reference.
- It also helps to arrange the components for a composition, as preparatory for a painting or for determining the values in a composition.
- Last, but not the least, sketching can be a joy on its own. Quite often, a pencil or pen-and-ink sketch has proved to be an independent picture in itself.

It is not just a matter of providing practice to our strokes, sketching gives a new depth of understanding to our eyes.

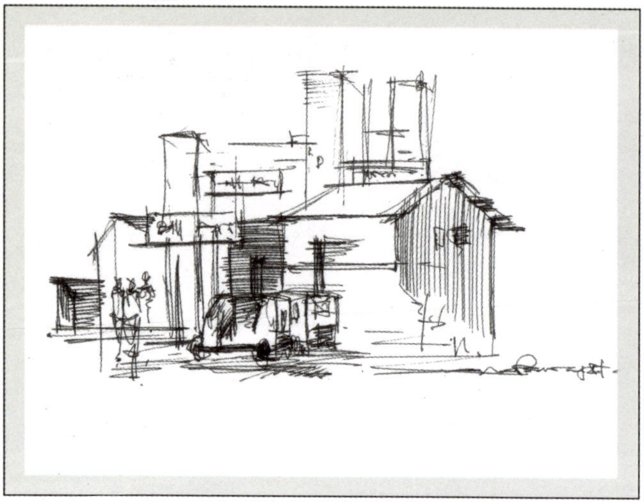

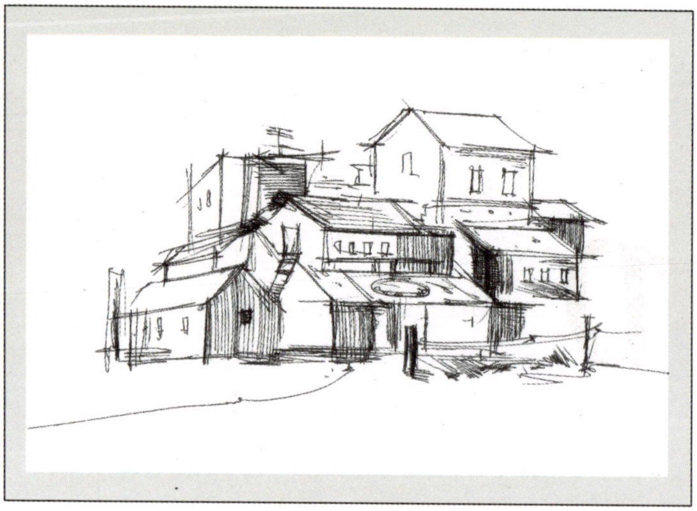

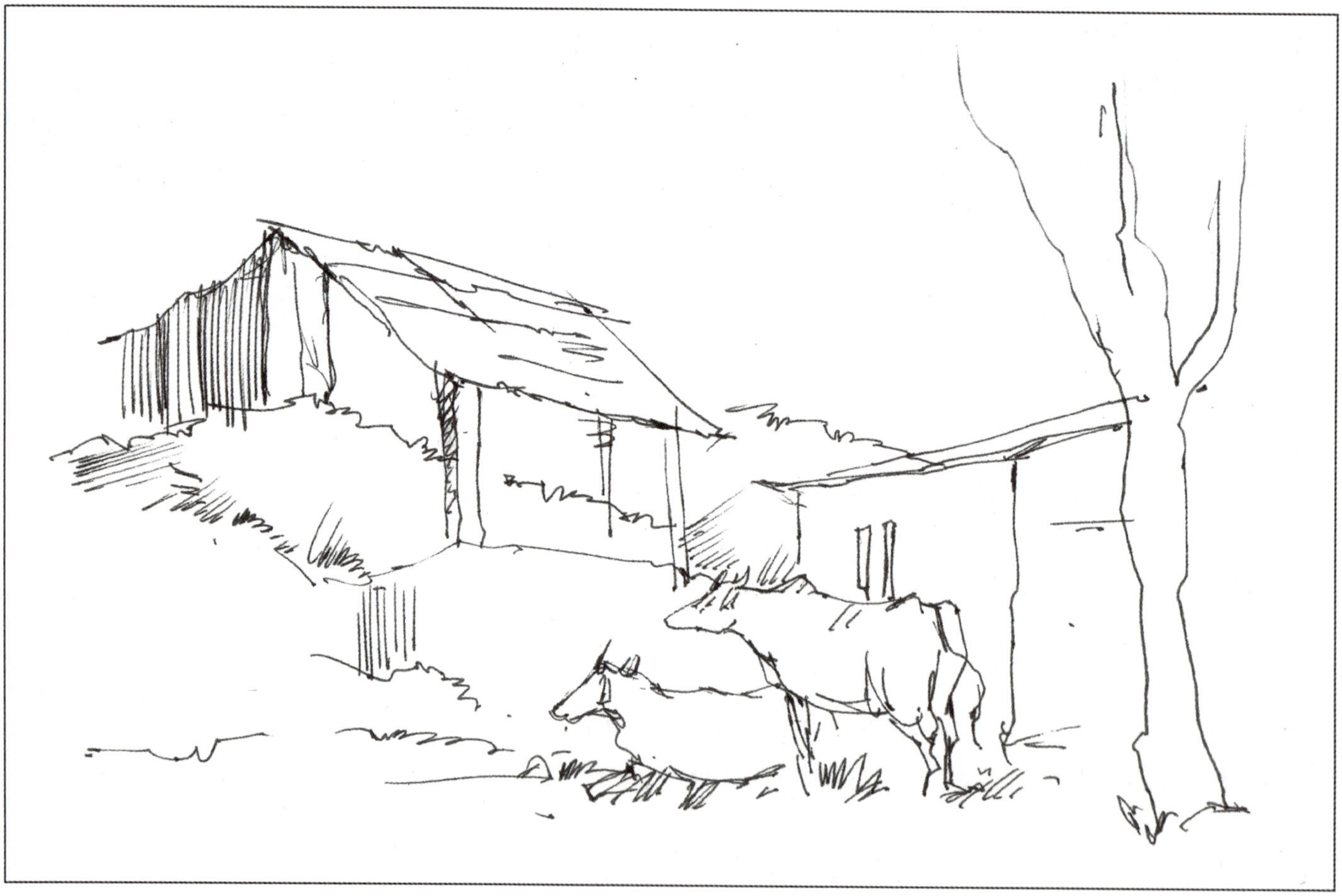

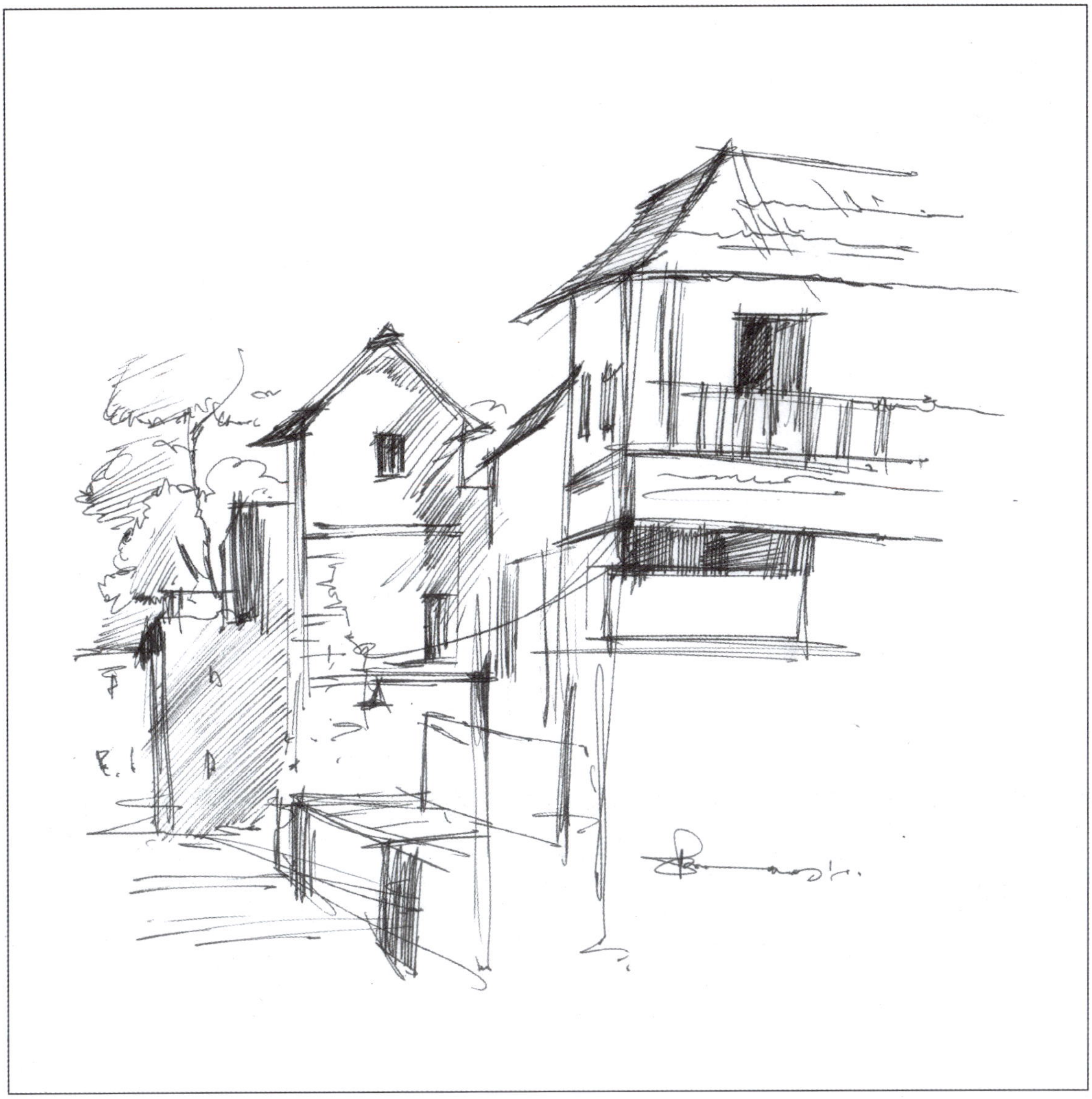

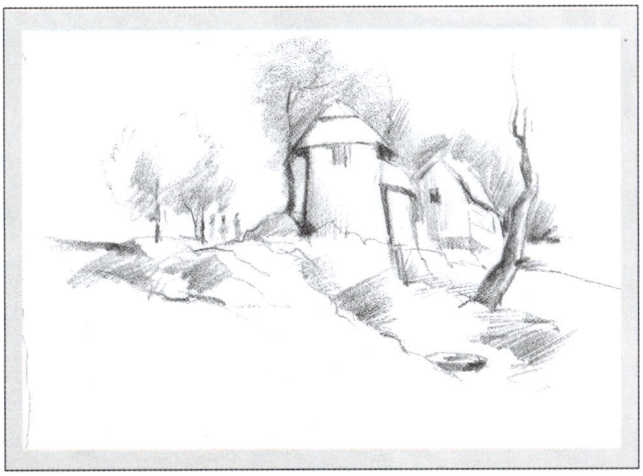

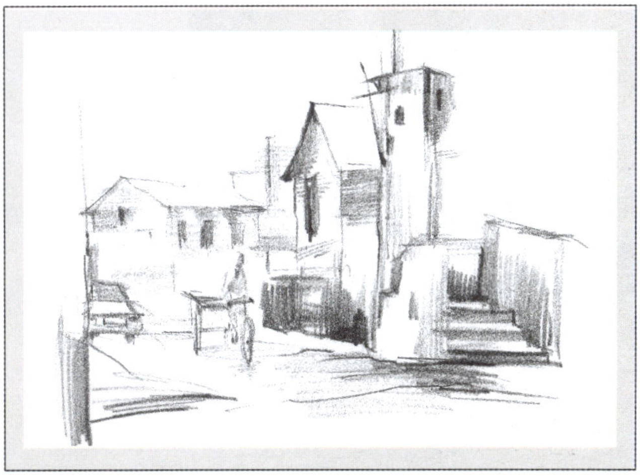

Composition

One would do well to remember that in painting we are not expected to exactly copy on paper all details that we see. Such a job could easily be done by a camera as well. A painting on the other hand should aim at being an independent work of art as a whole, with a beauty of its own that is more than the sum of its parts. Merely by faithfulness to details every photograph does not become a work of art. It is the arrangement of the elements in a particular way that adds the touch of beauty to a picture.

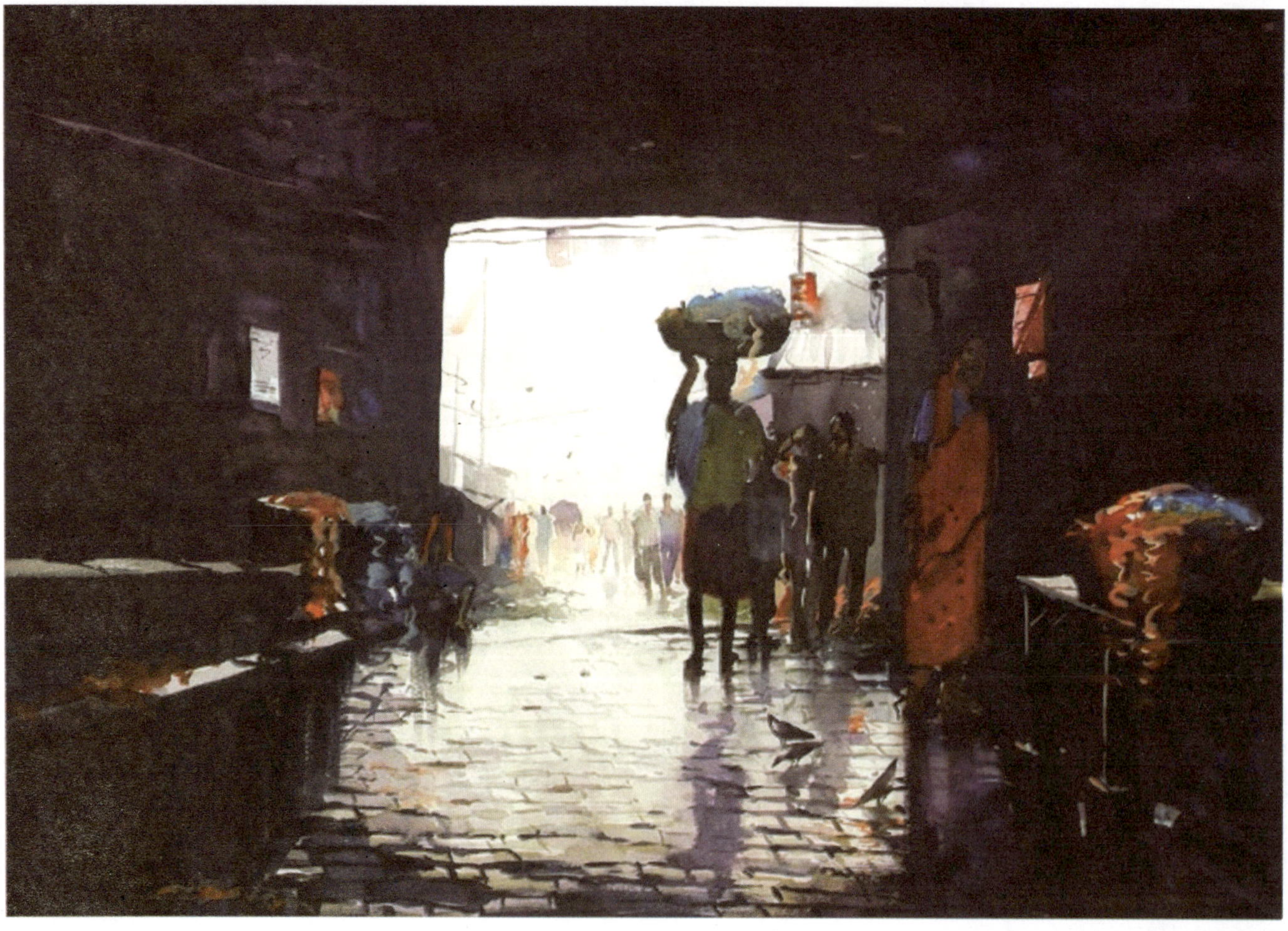

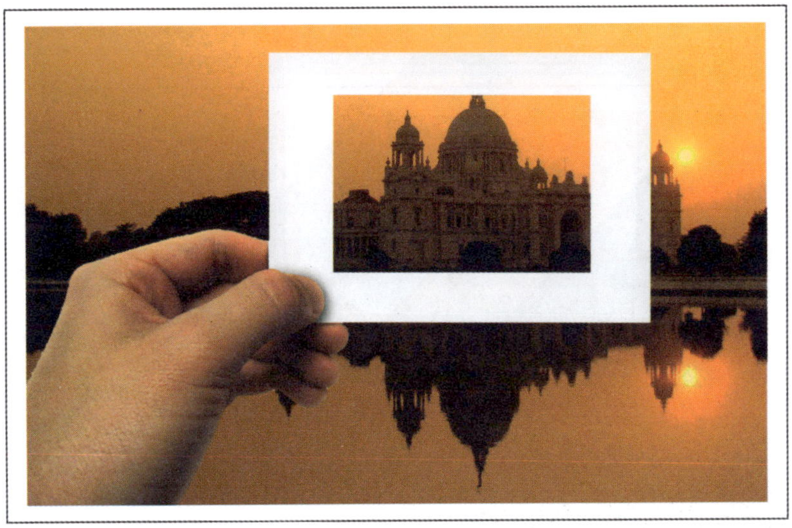

Learning to draw is not only about mastering the ability to draw what you see, but knowing how to create a balanced and harmonious composition within the borders of your page is also an integral part of making art.

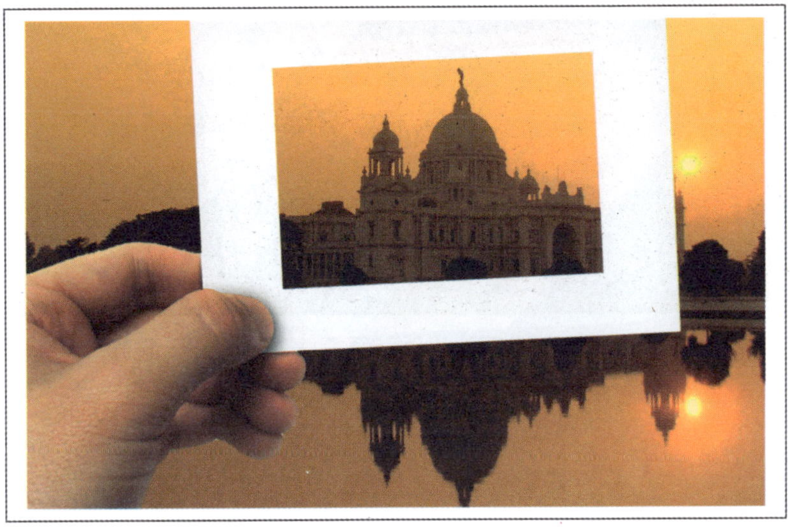

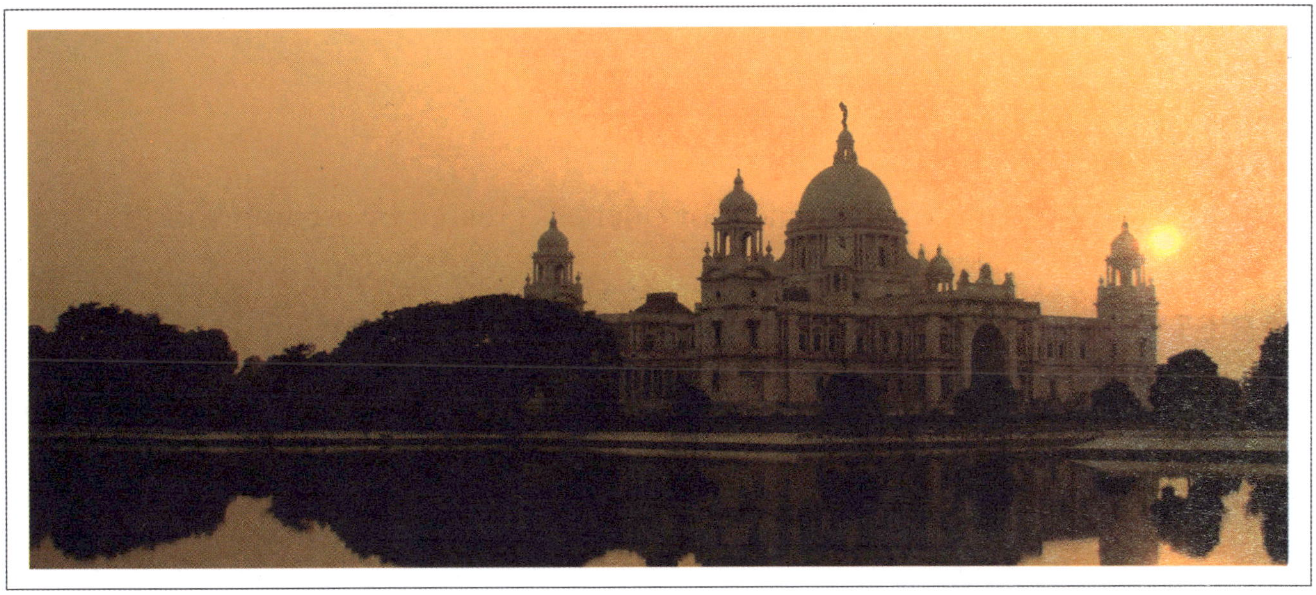

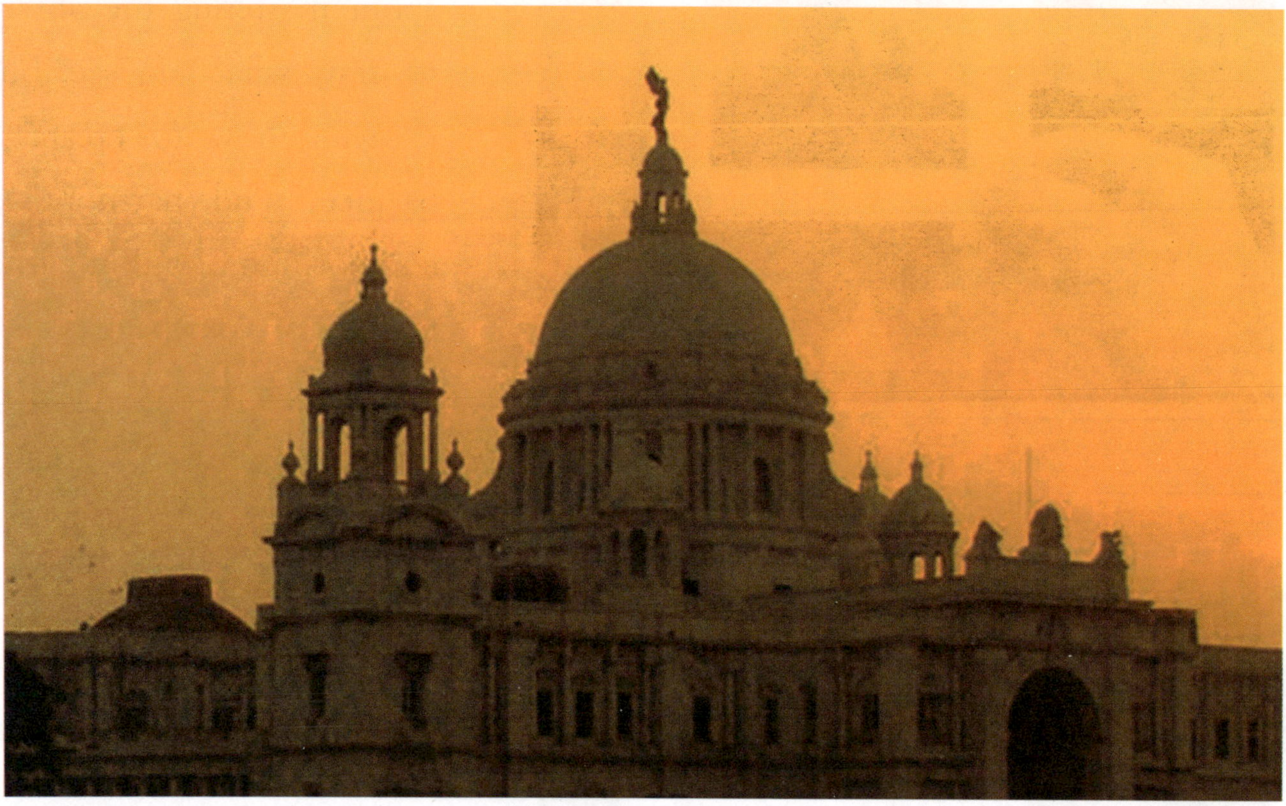

MOVEMENT

This refers to the way your eye moves through the composition. You can create dynamic or static movement depending on your intent.

HARMONY

Harmony is the quality of wholeness or oneness created by a composition.

VARIETY

Variety is having different forms or types within a composition. These differences can create visual and conceptual interests.

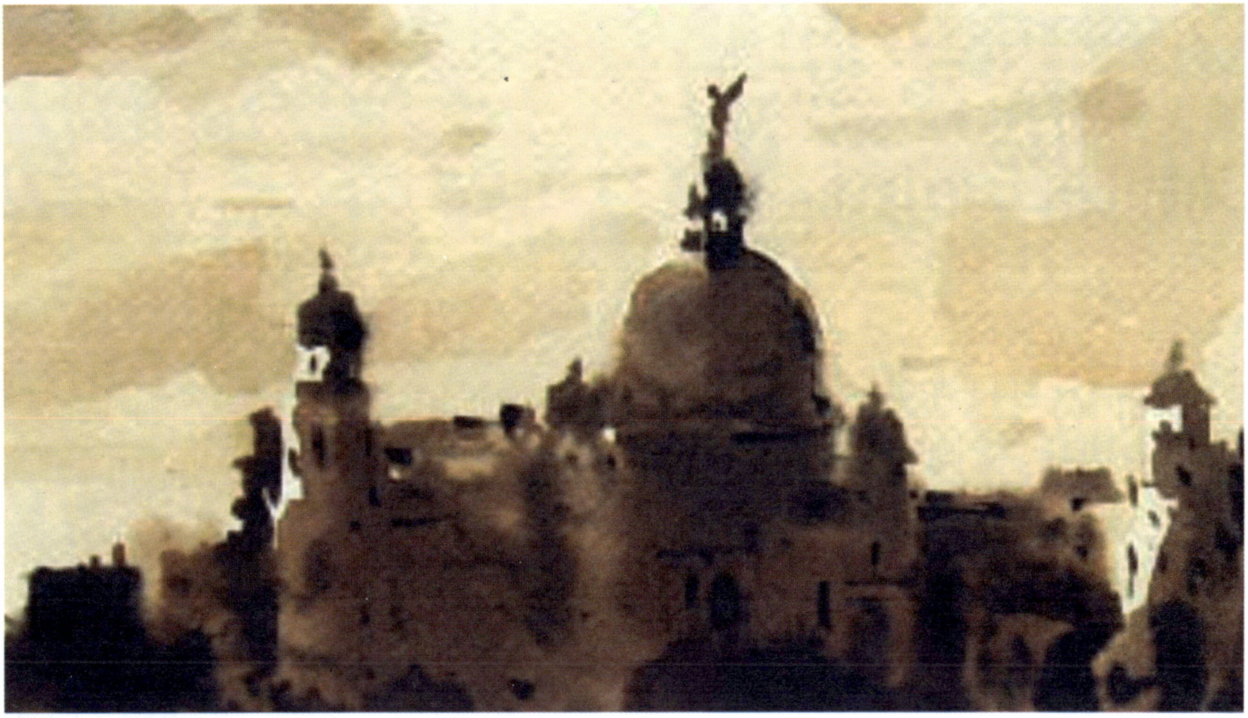

BALANCE

This refers to arranging a composition so that no one part overpowers or feels heavier than another part.

FOCAL POINT

It is creating a point of interest within a composition that attracts the viewers' eye.

CONTRAST

It refers to the difference in values within a composition. Low contrast would include a shallow range of values while high contrast ranges from black to white.

PROPORTION

It refers to the size and space relationships of all elements within a composition. It can be used to create the illusion of largeness or smallness in an artwork.

❏❏❏

Let Us Paint

We should look at the scene. Here, it is expected that we don't focus on any particular part, nor should we get involved in any detail. In fact, we should forget about the individual separate identities of components such as a tree, a house etc., it will help us see them as larger shapes. This process is facilitated by thinking of the scene as two-dimensional, and by viewing such a scene, identifying the form becomes easy. Often a particular mass strikes us and then around this centre of attraction we can start composing the picture. Two/three compositions should then be quickly made. First we can make small sketches of composition – here the forms should be drawn as simple ones, also their number should be kept to a minimum. This makes it easier to compose the picture from it.

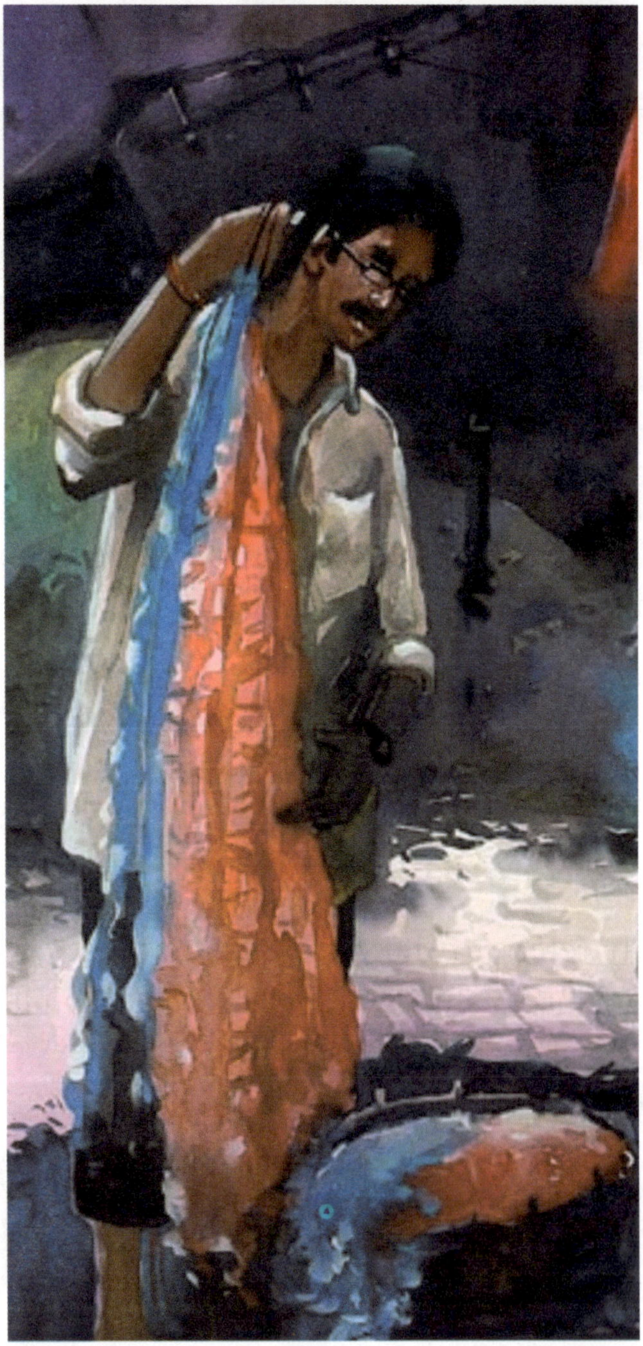

Often, after we have practiced considerably, a particular play of light and shade or a colour-scheme strikes us with its interesting possibilities. On such occasions, without spending any time in thinking etc., the fleeting impression should first be captured on paper immediately. In that heightened state of excitement, there is more likelihood of our catching the impression satisfactorily.

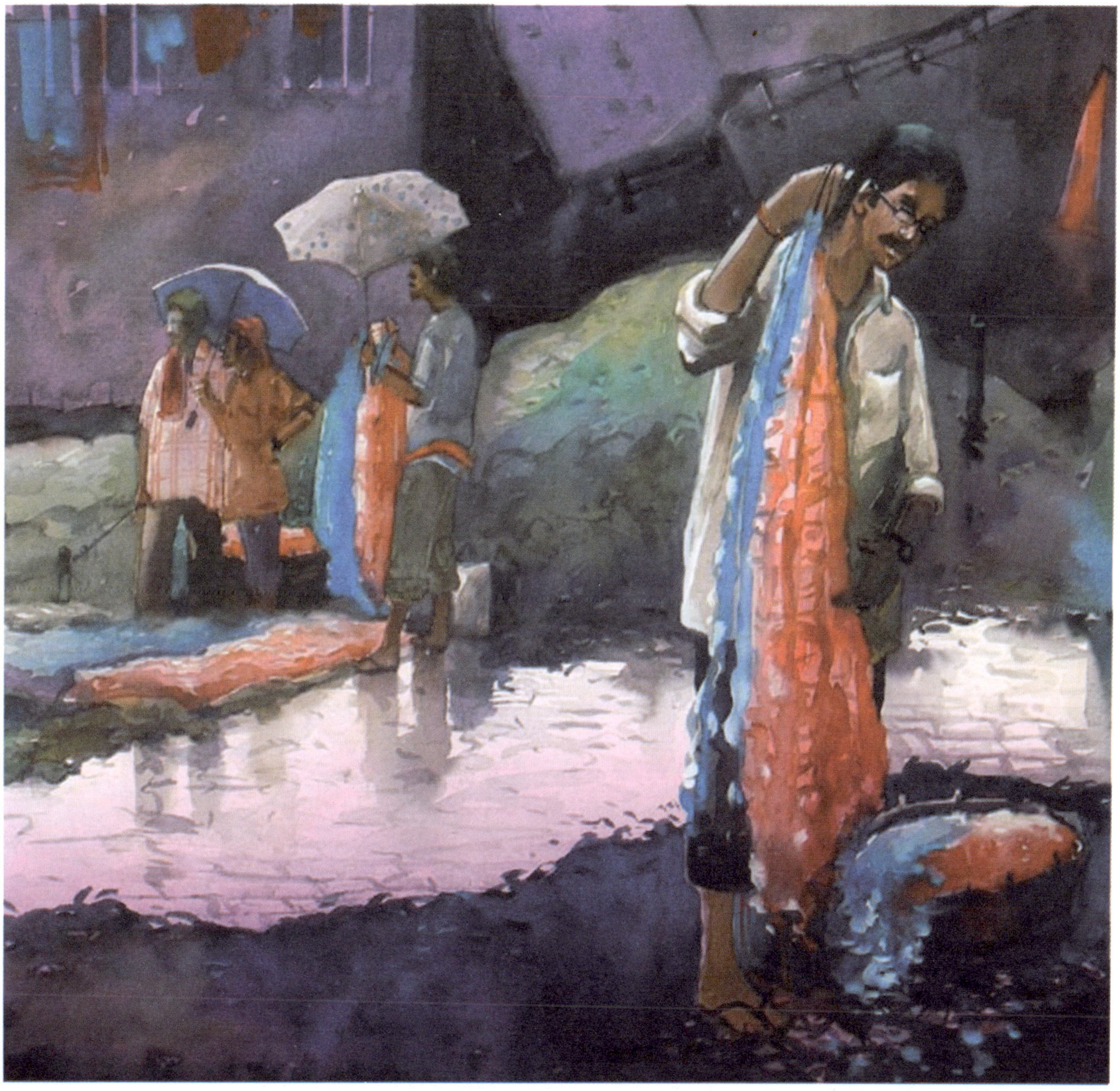

❑❑❑

Demonstration 1

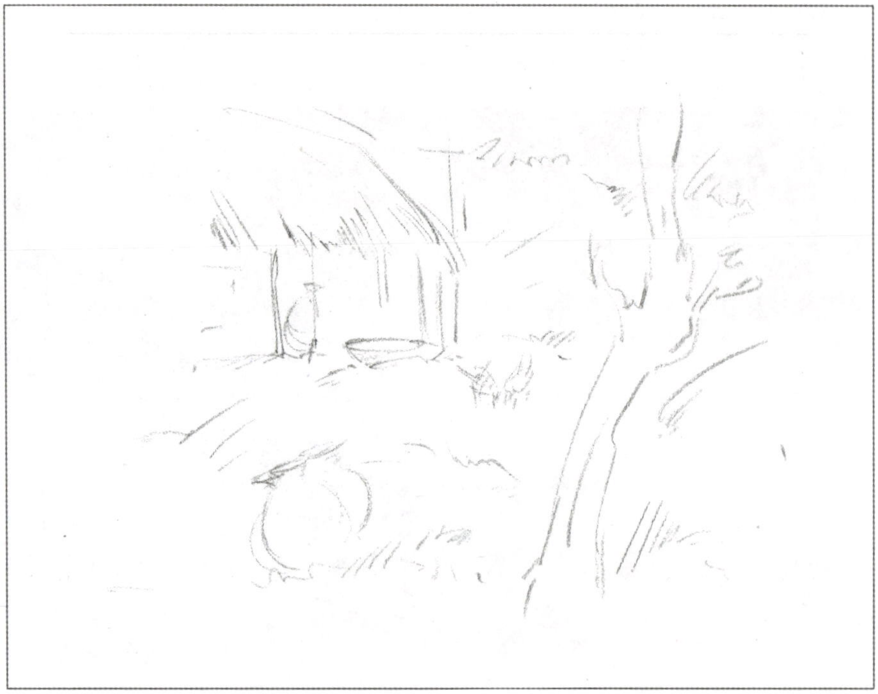

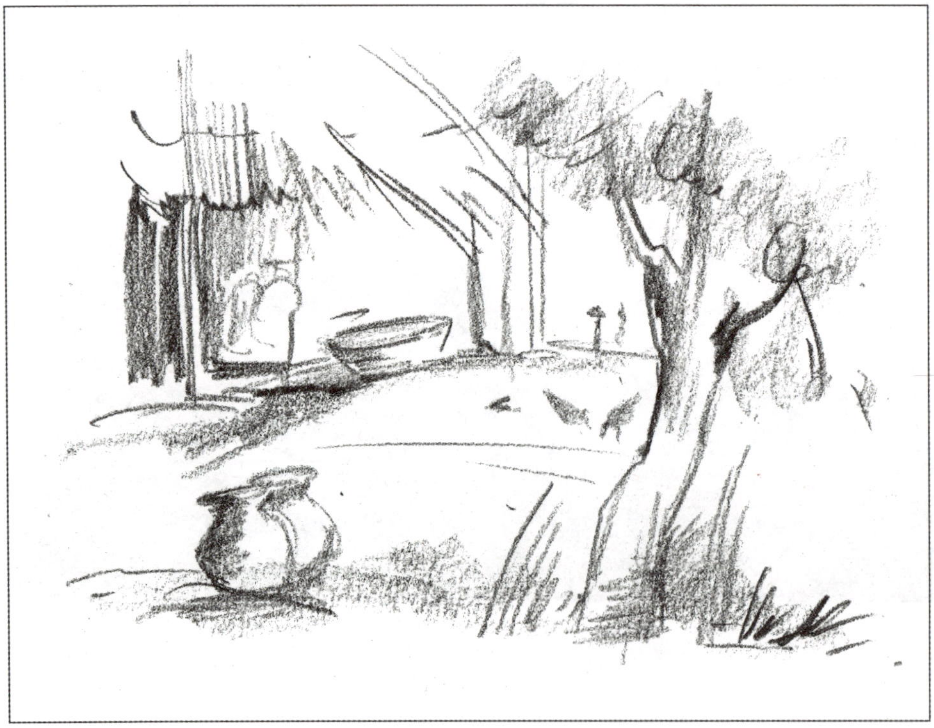

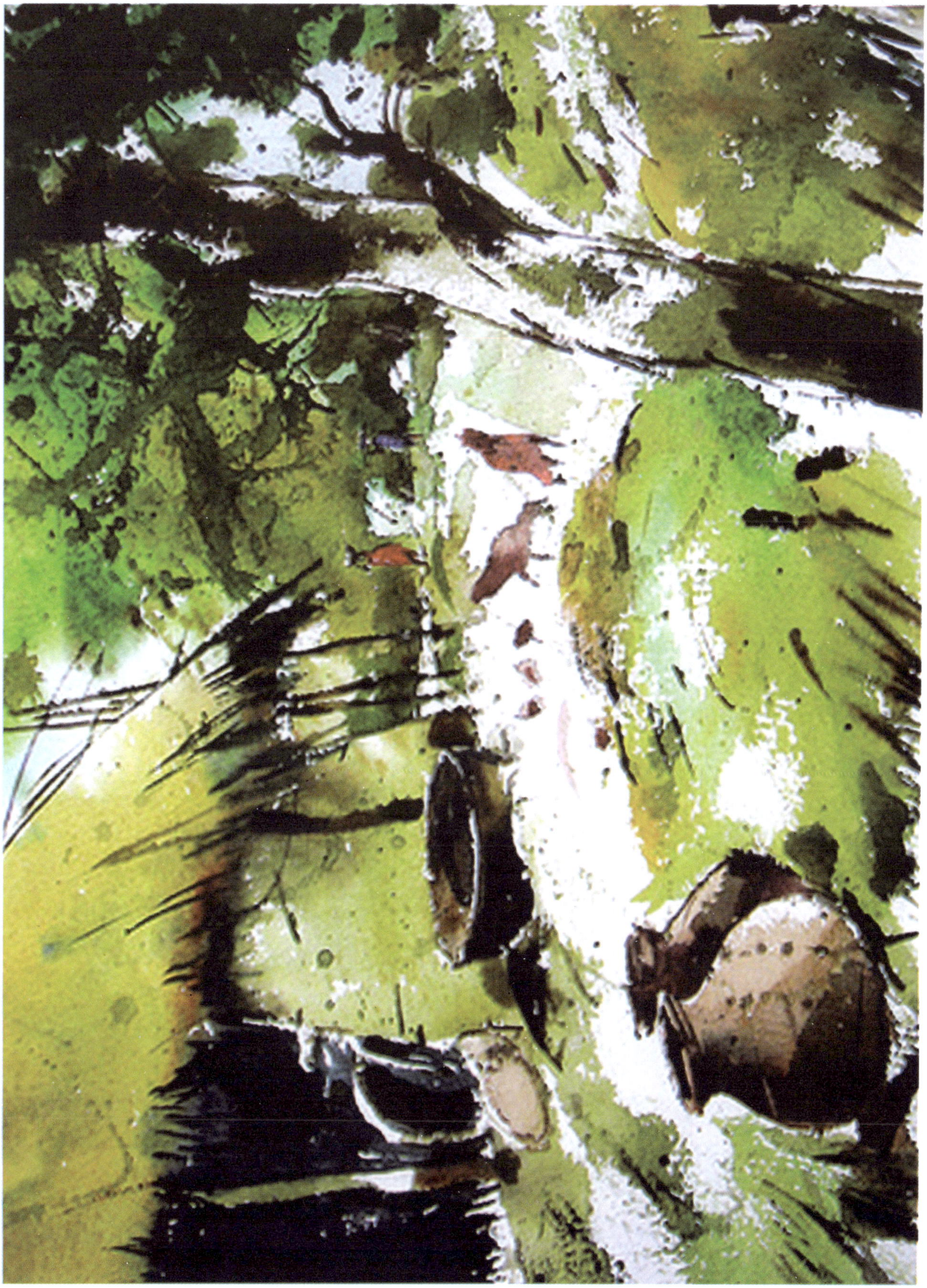

Demonstration 2

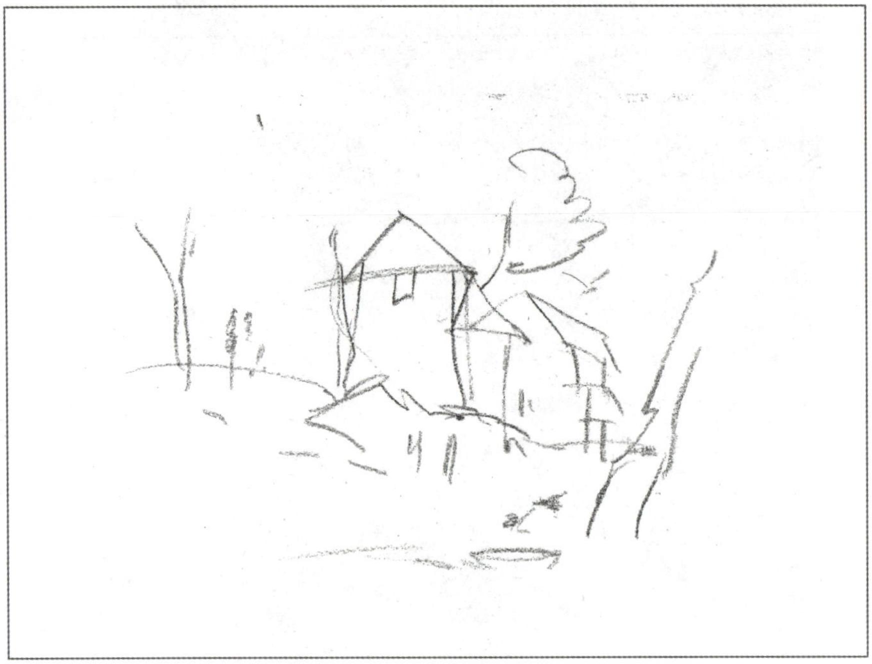

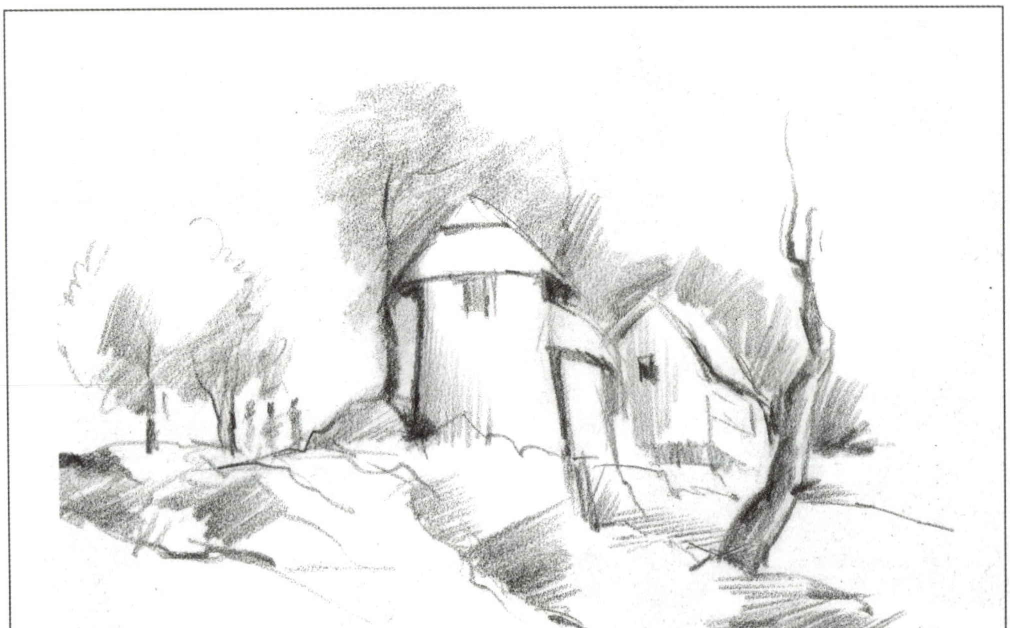

The shadows in the morning are lighter, and the morning atmosphere, too, has a faint, bluish tinge. At such times, the light greyish shadow also gets a blue tinge. So to paint a morning in a picture, the light should be made slightly bluish, and the grey of the shadow should also be mixed with a little blue.

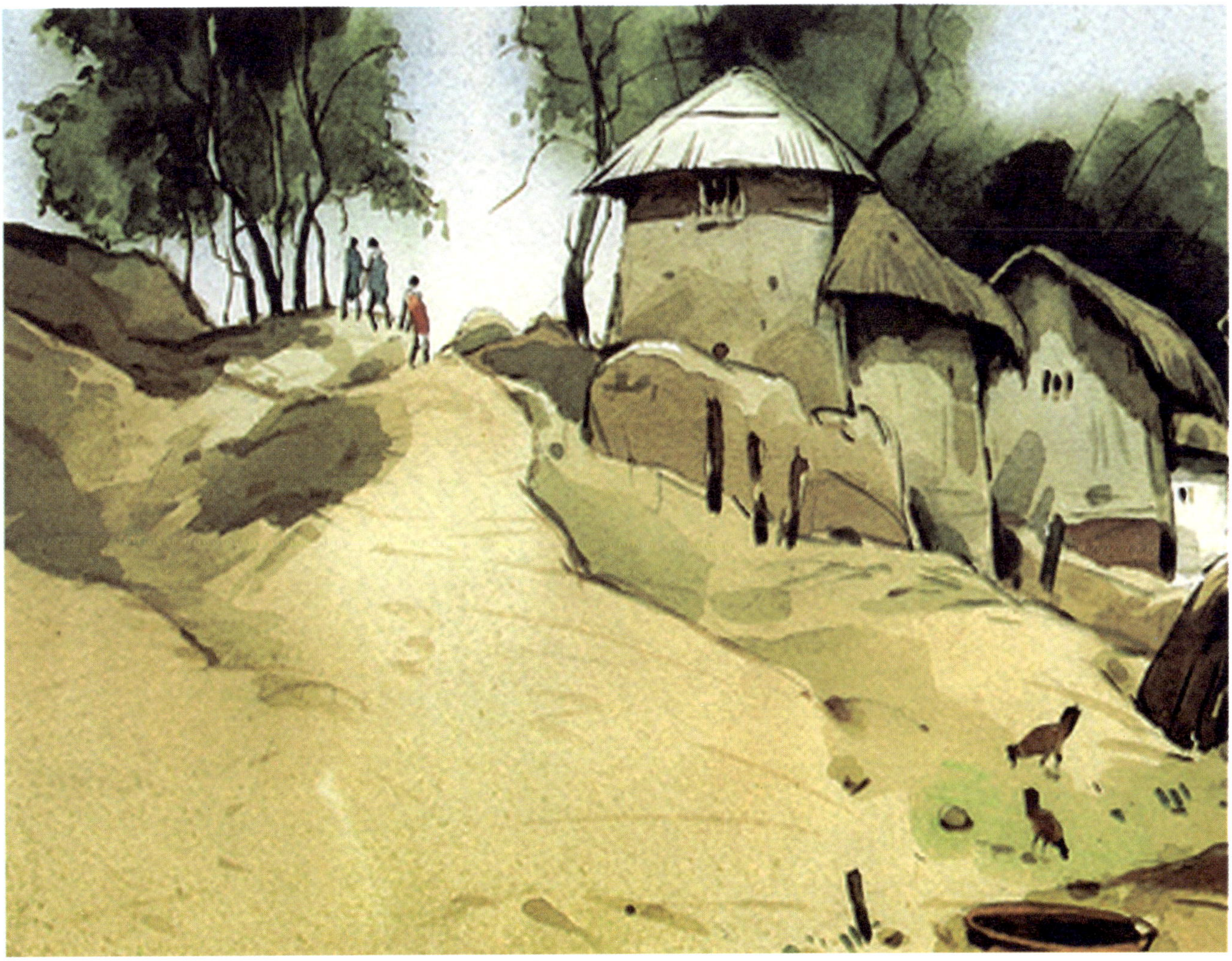

Demonstration 3

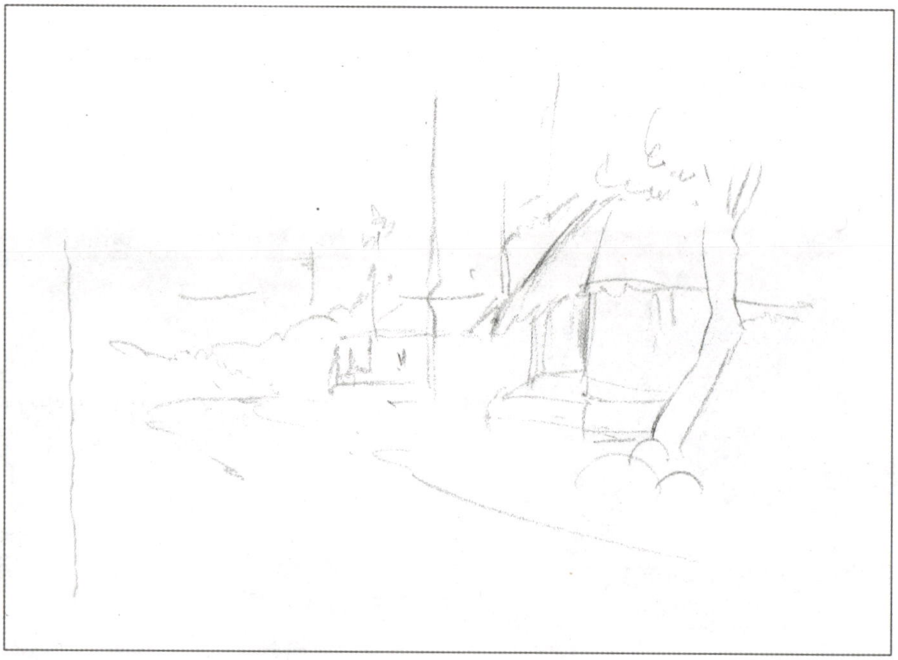

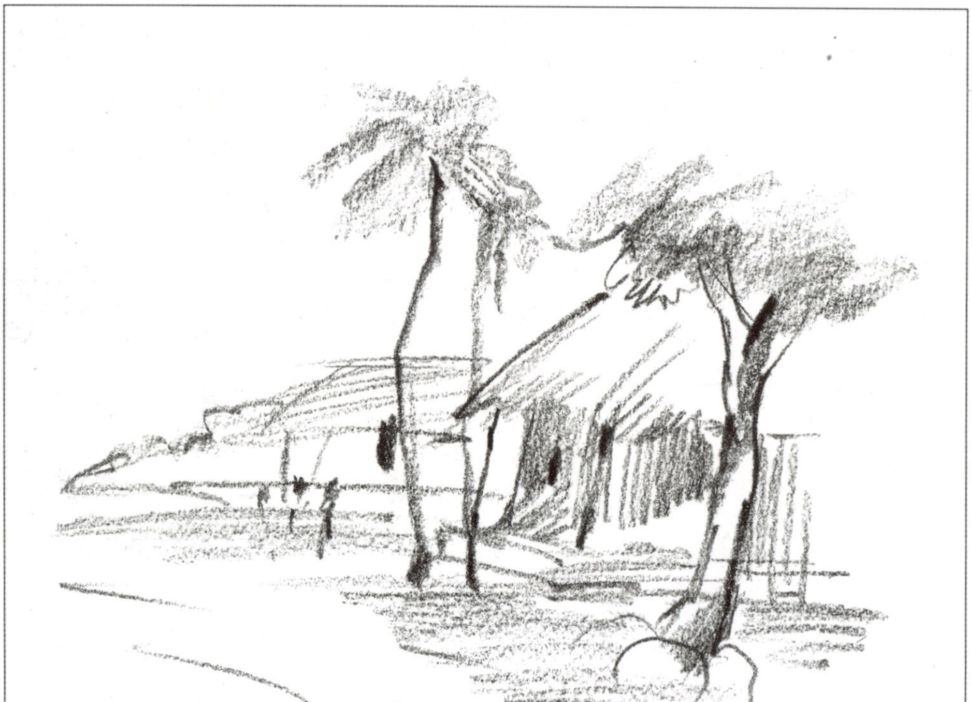

Though shadow means less light or total absence of light, it doesn't mean absence of colours. The shadow, too, has its own colours and these various shades of colour come in handy to depict a mood and the time of the painting. We should observe the shadows of various objects falling at different times, noting how the shapes and colours of the shadows go on changing.

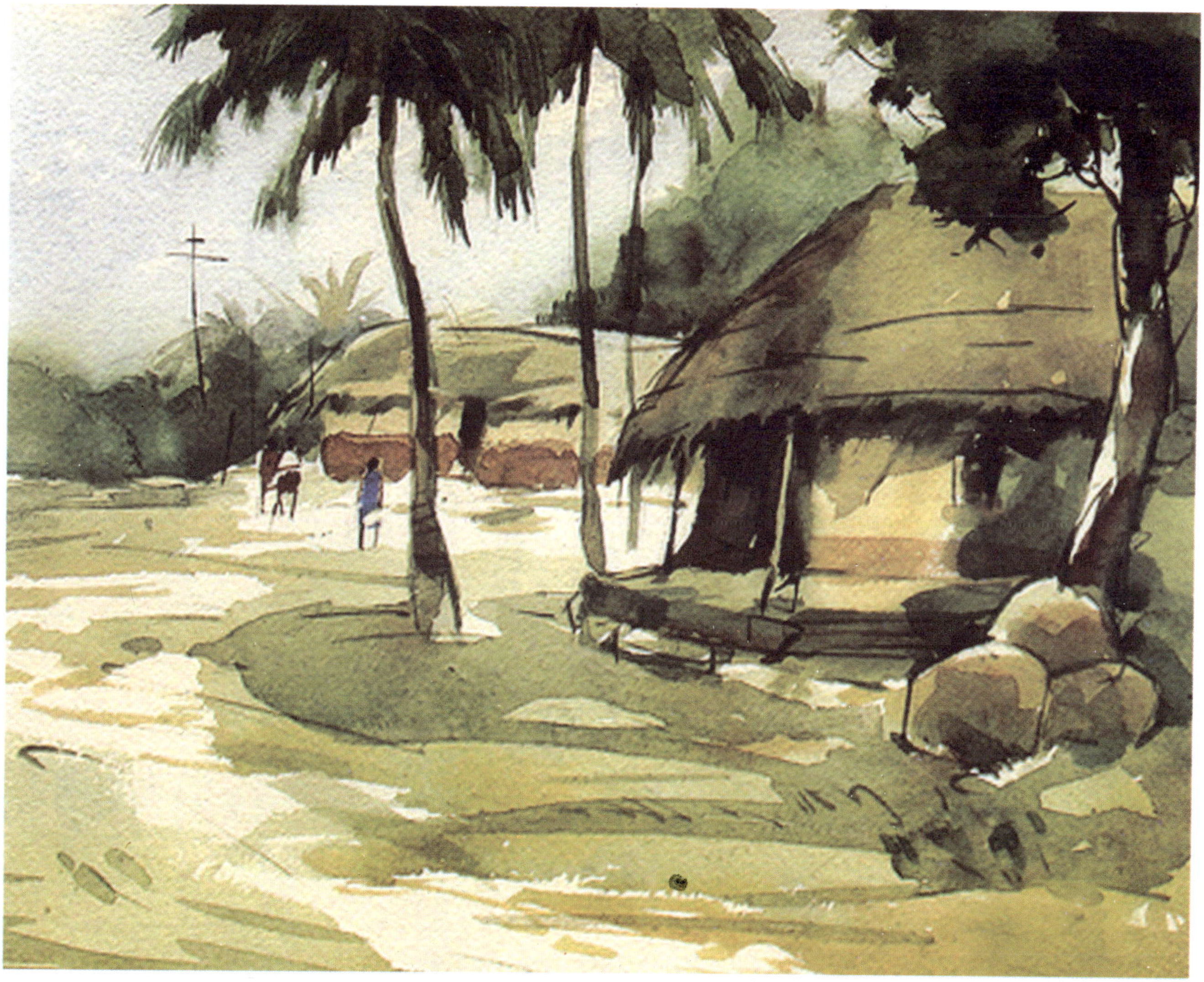

❑❑❑

Gallery

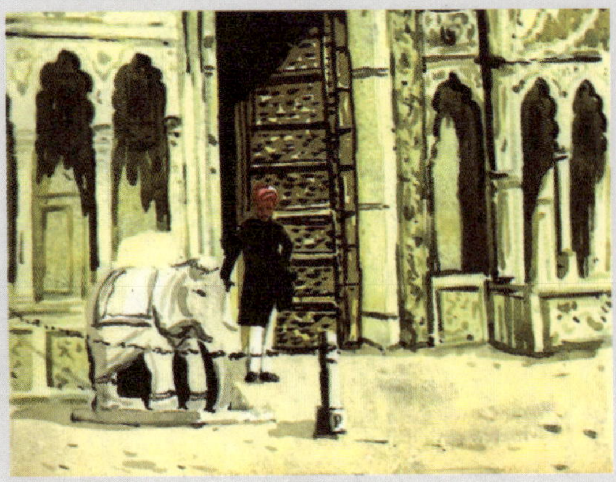

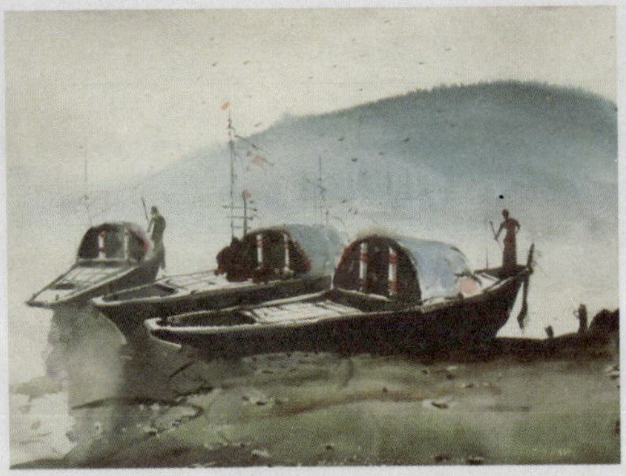

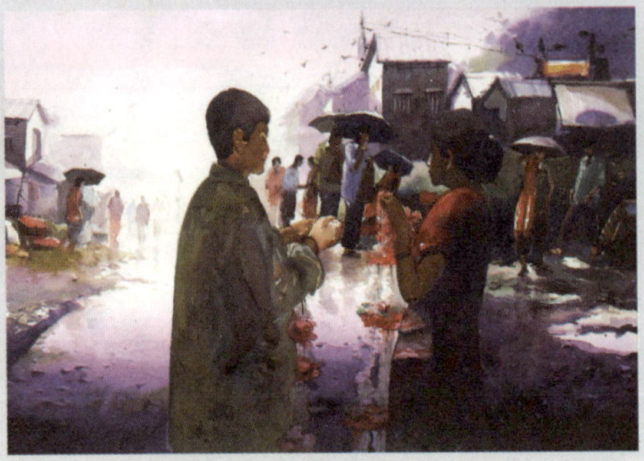

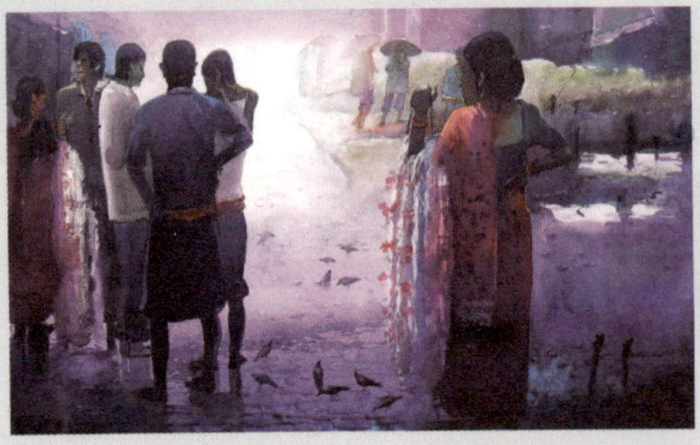

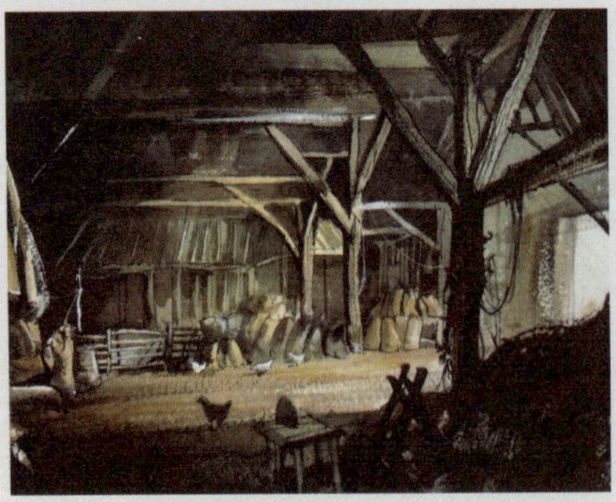

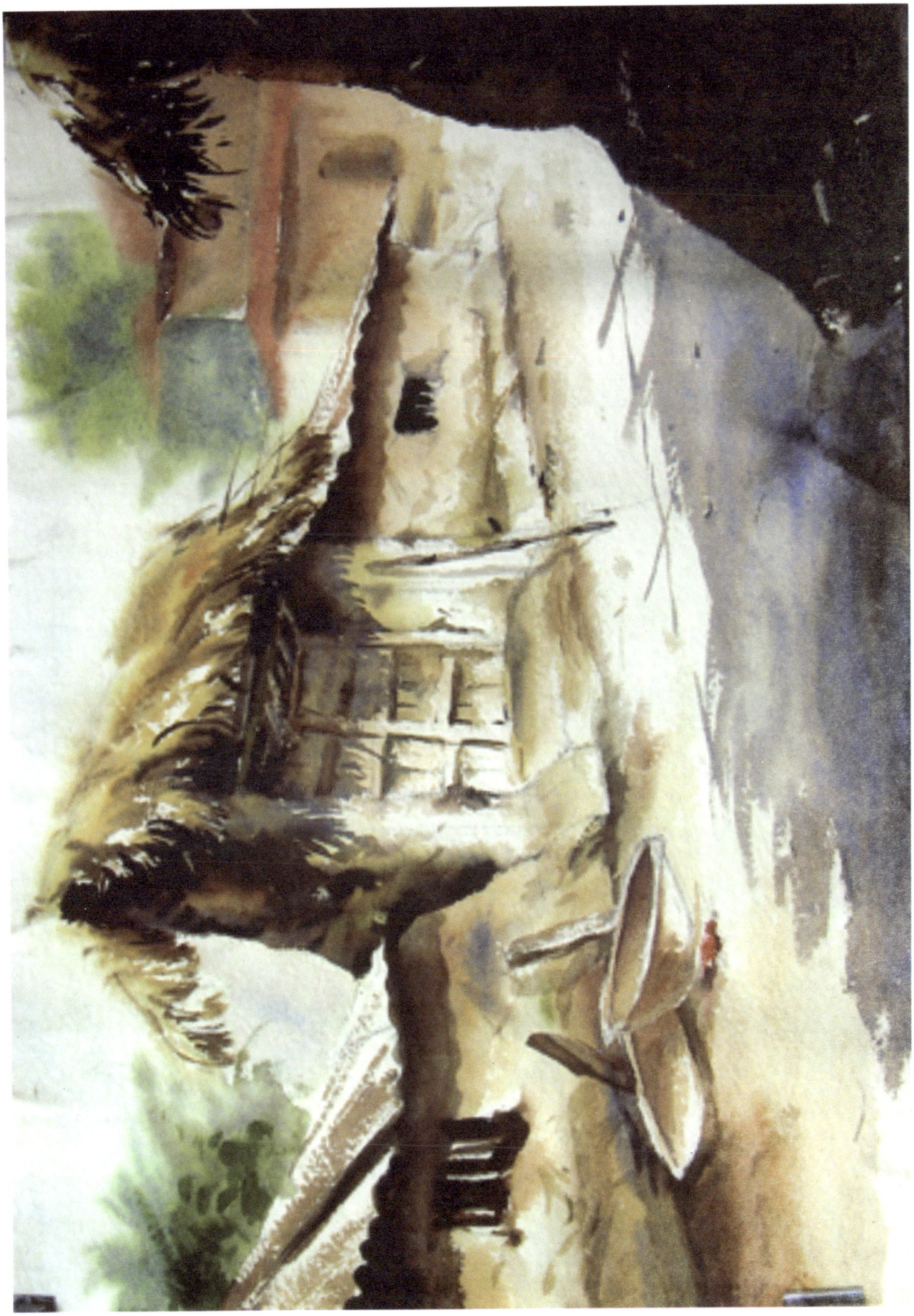

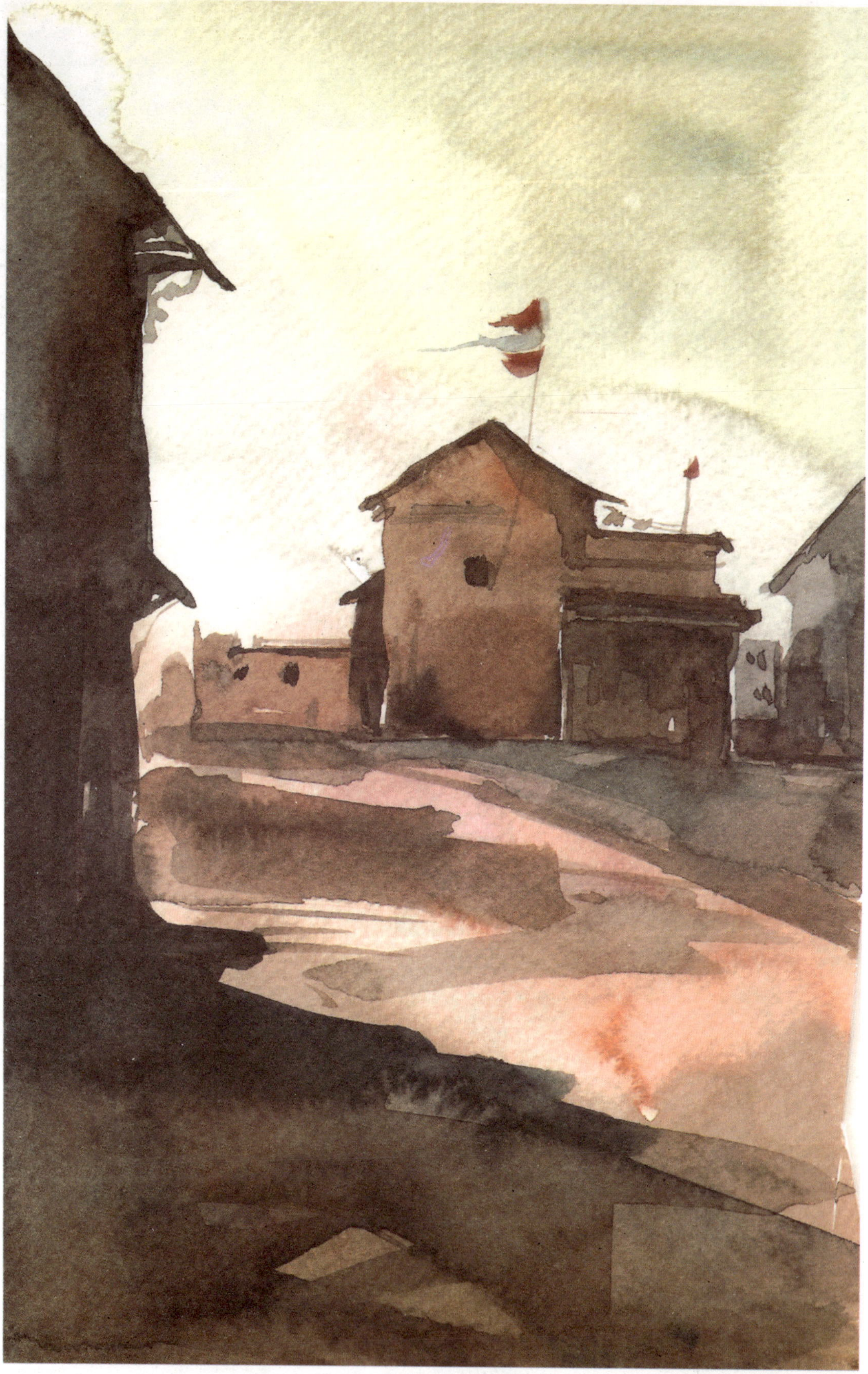

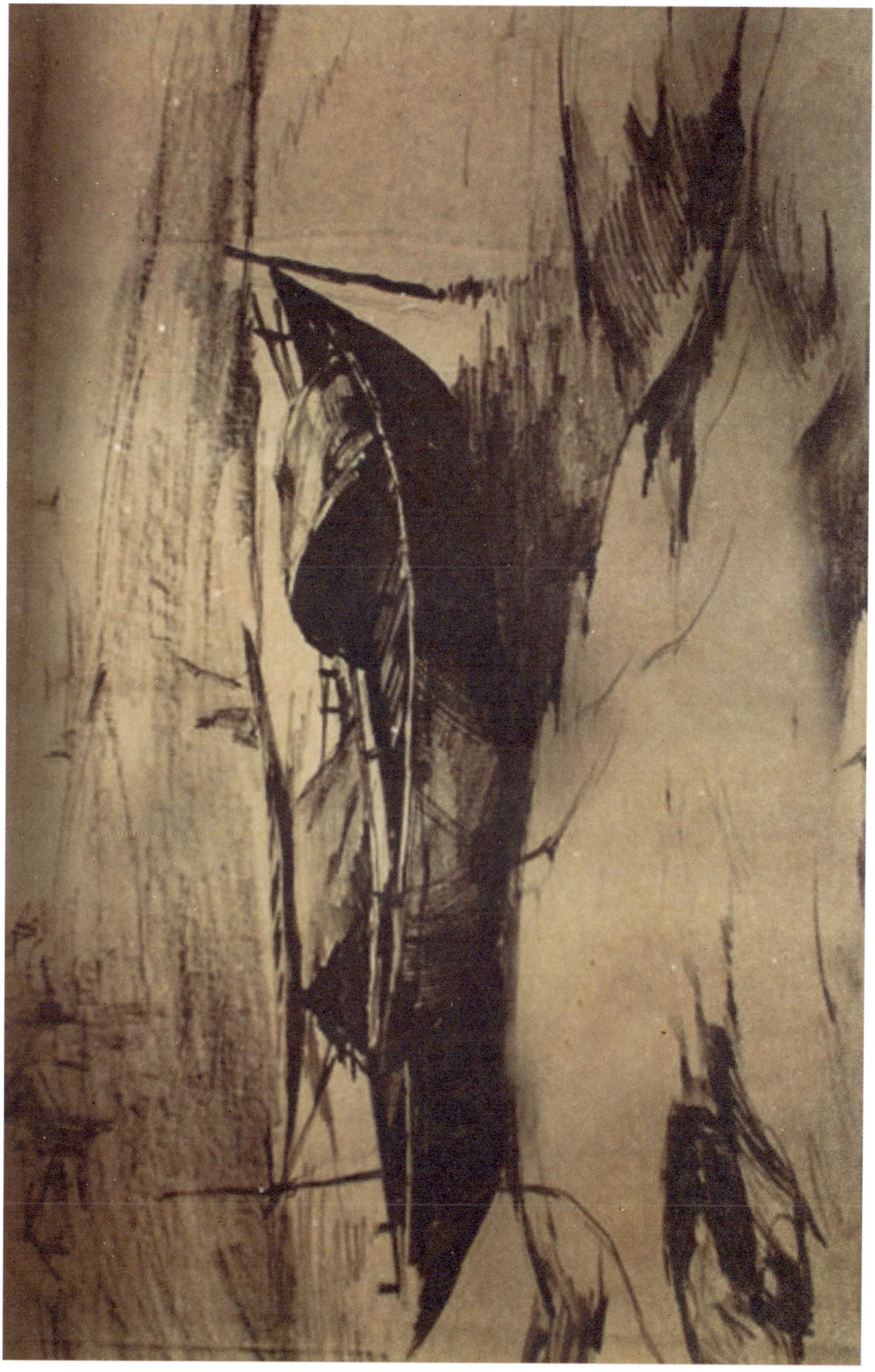

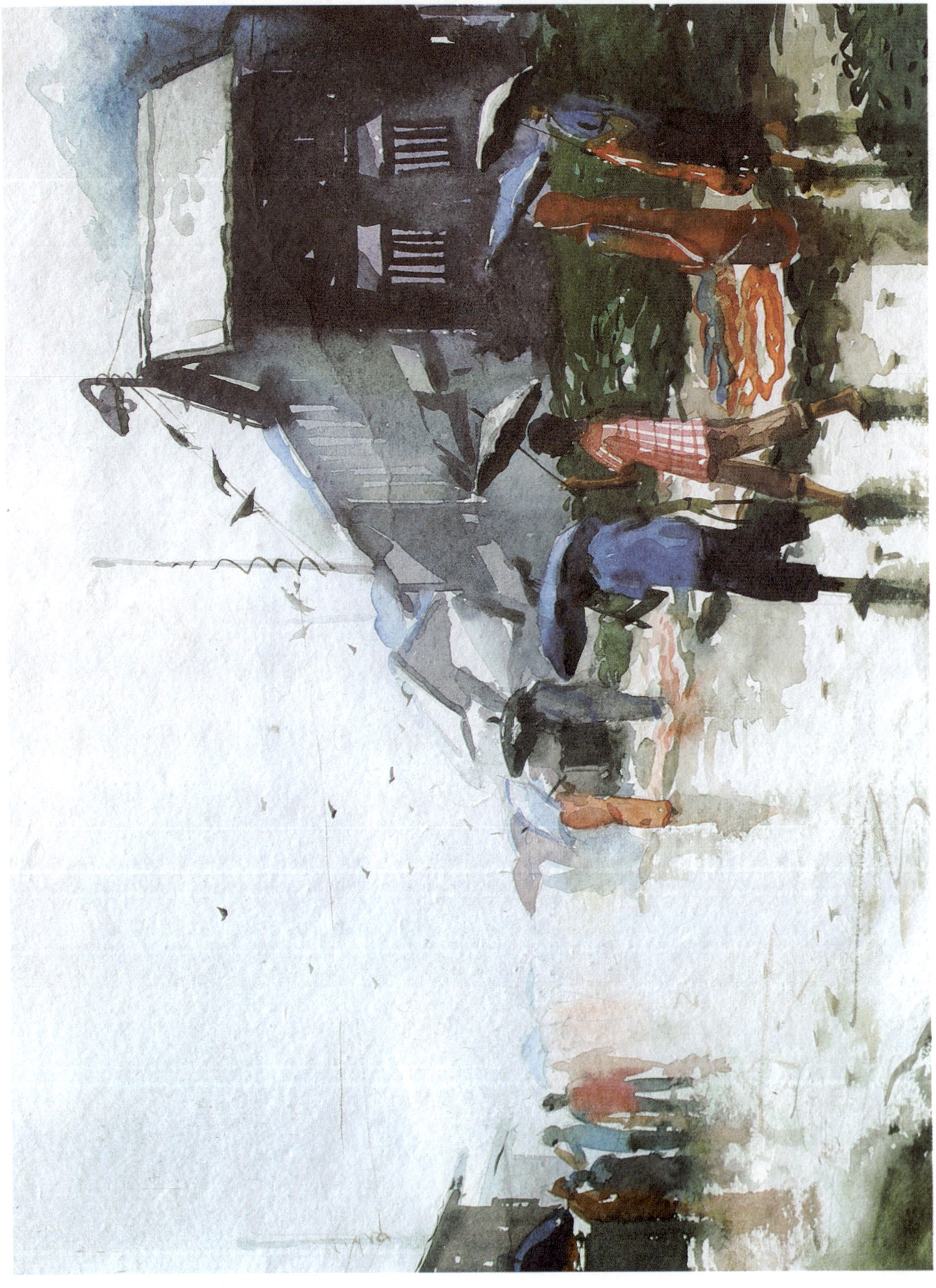

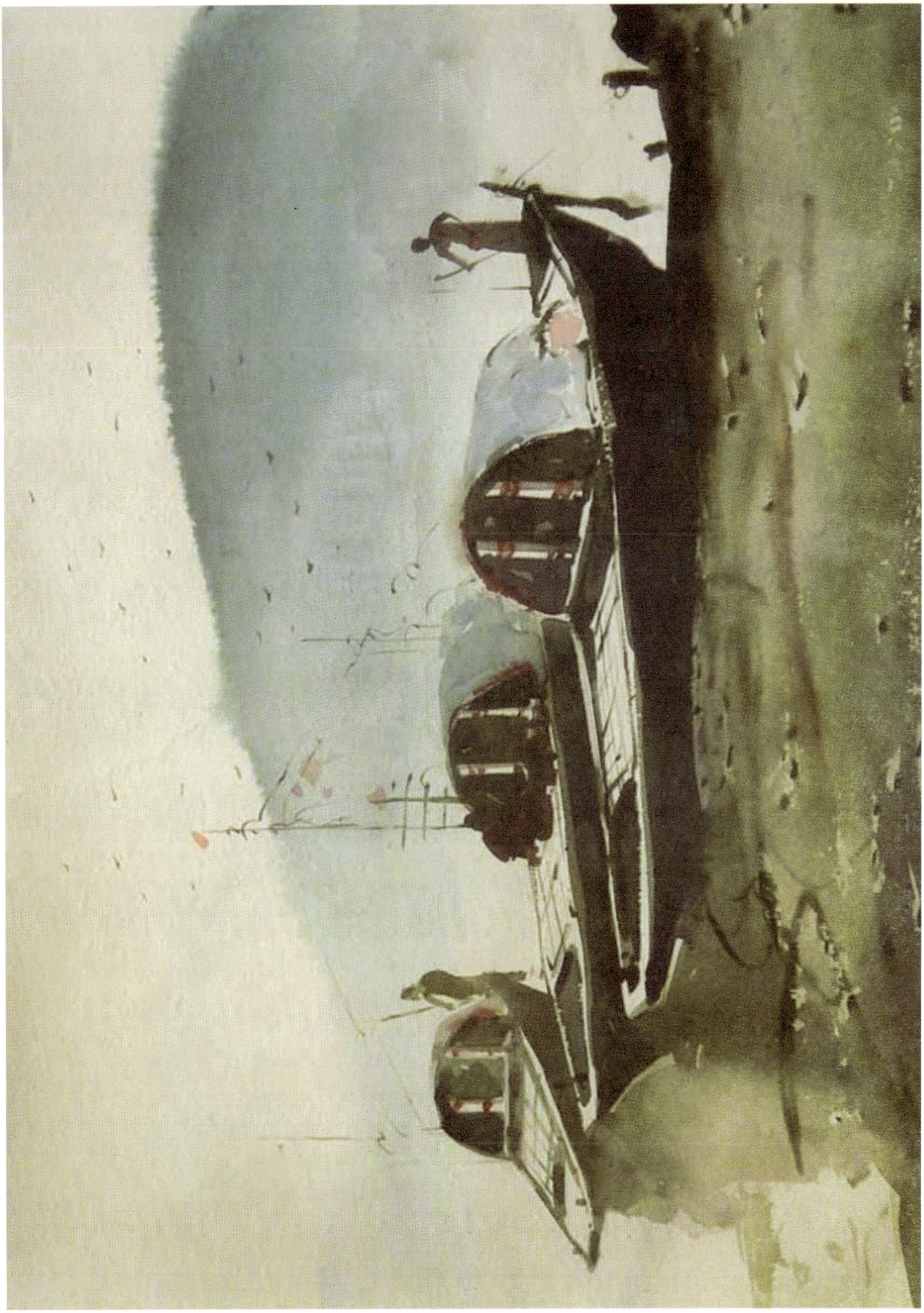

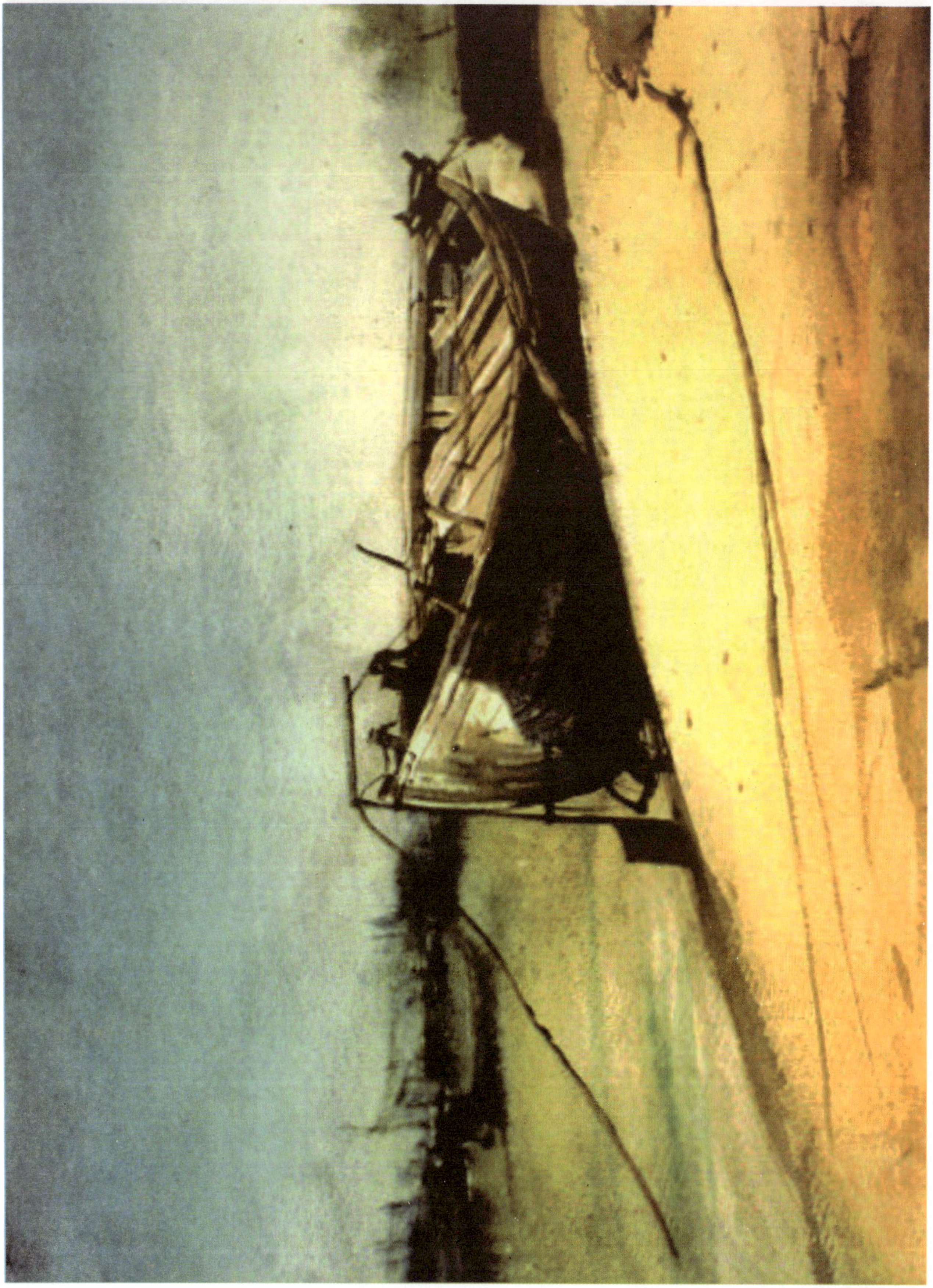

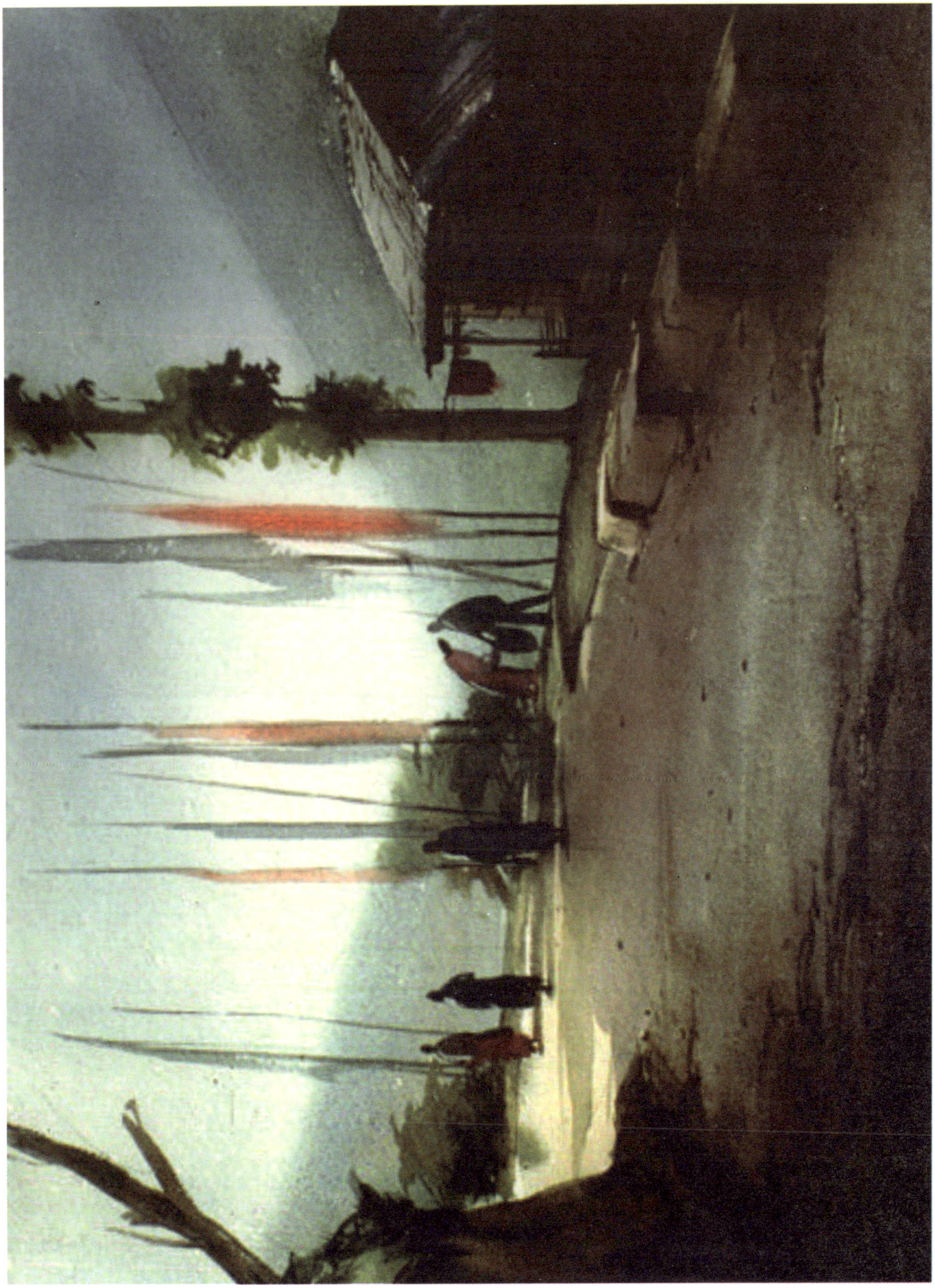

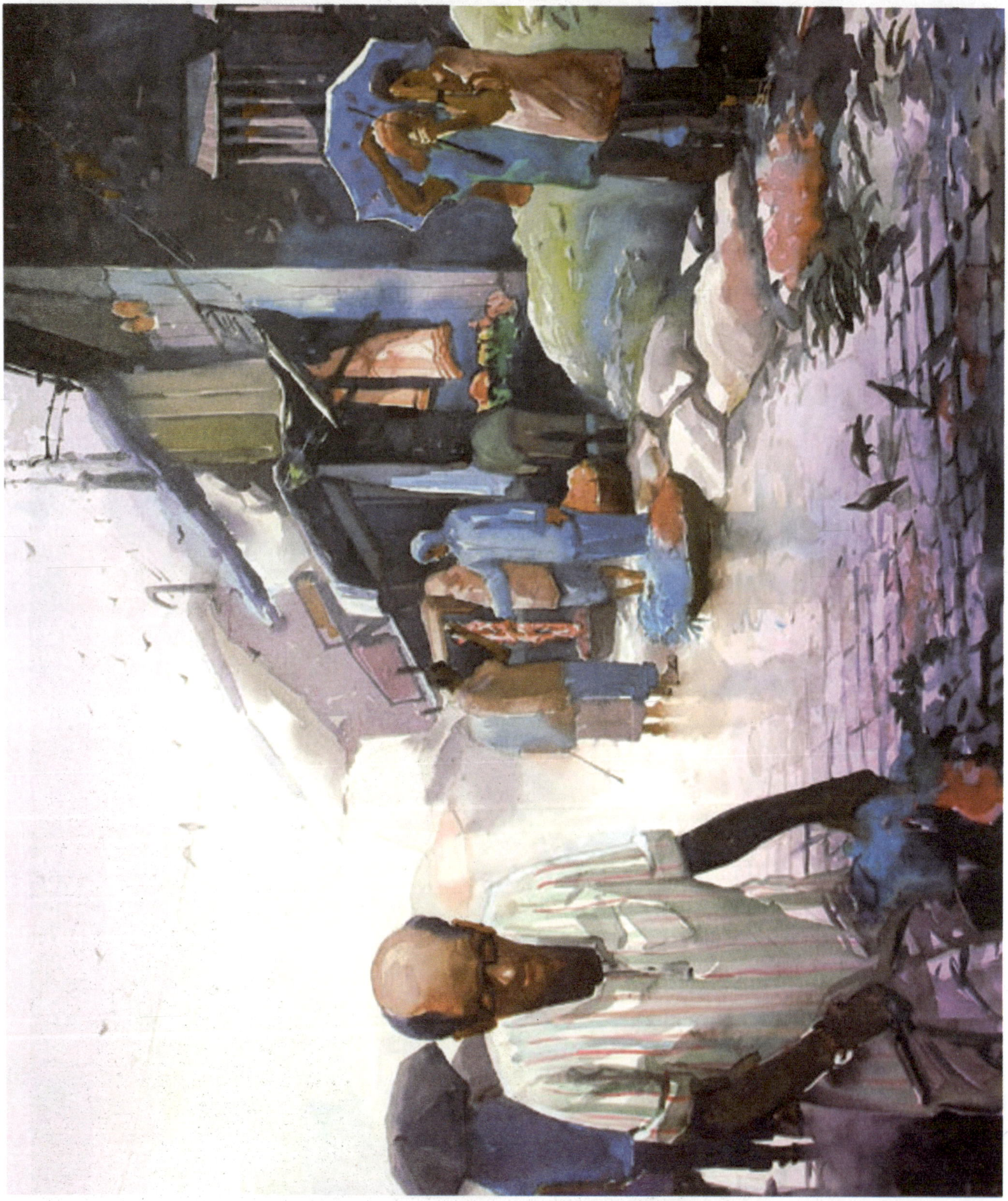

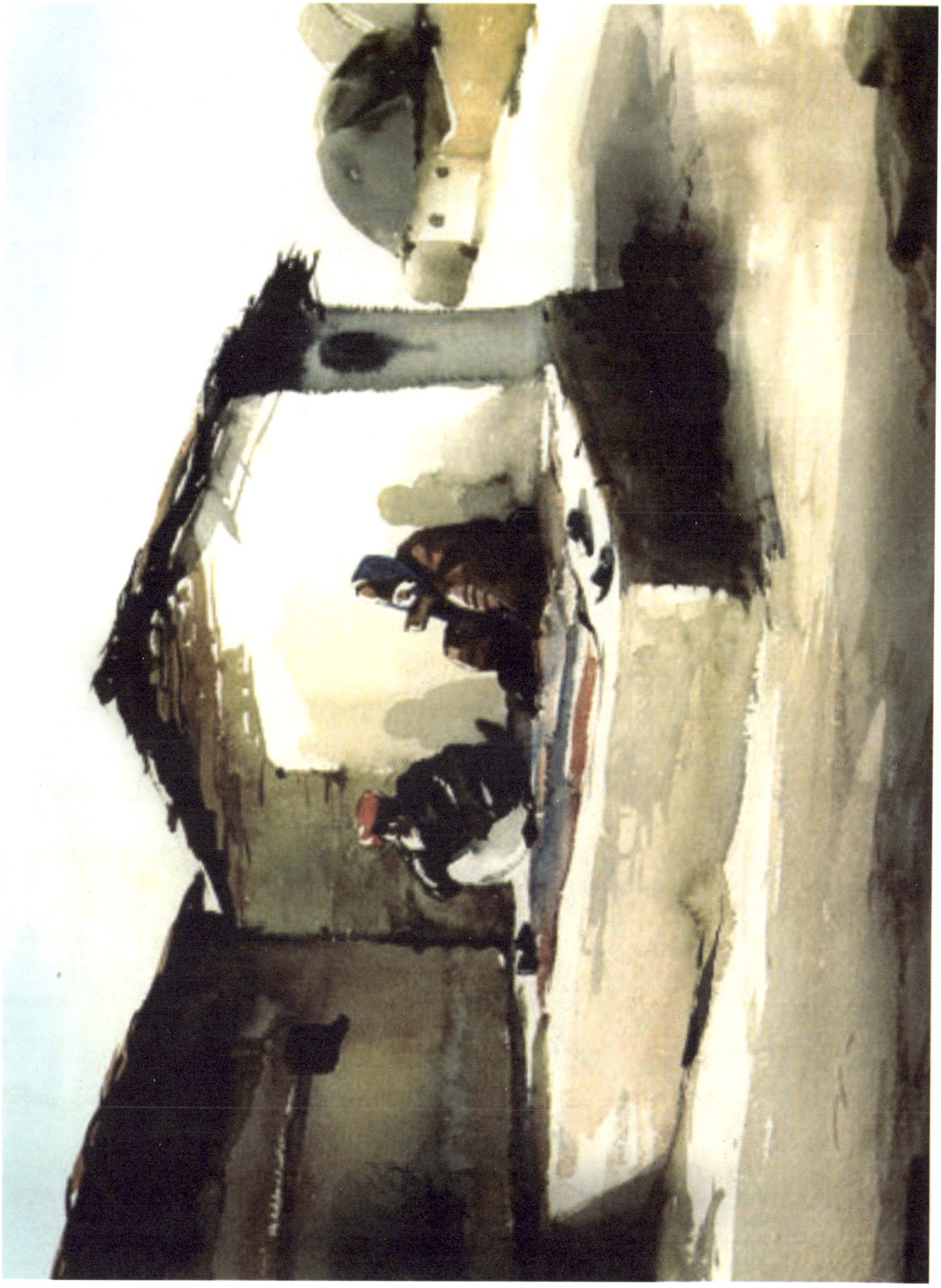

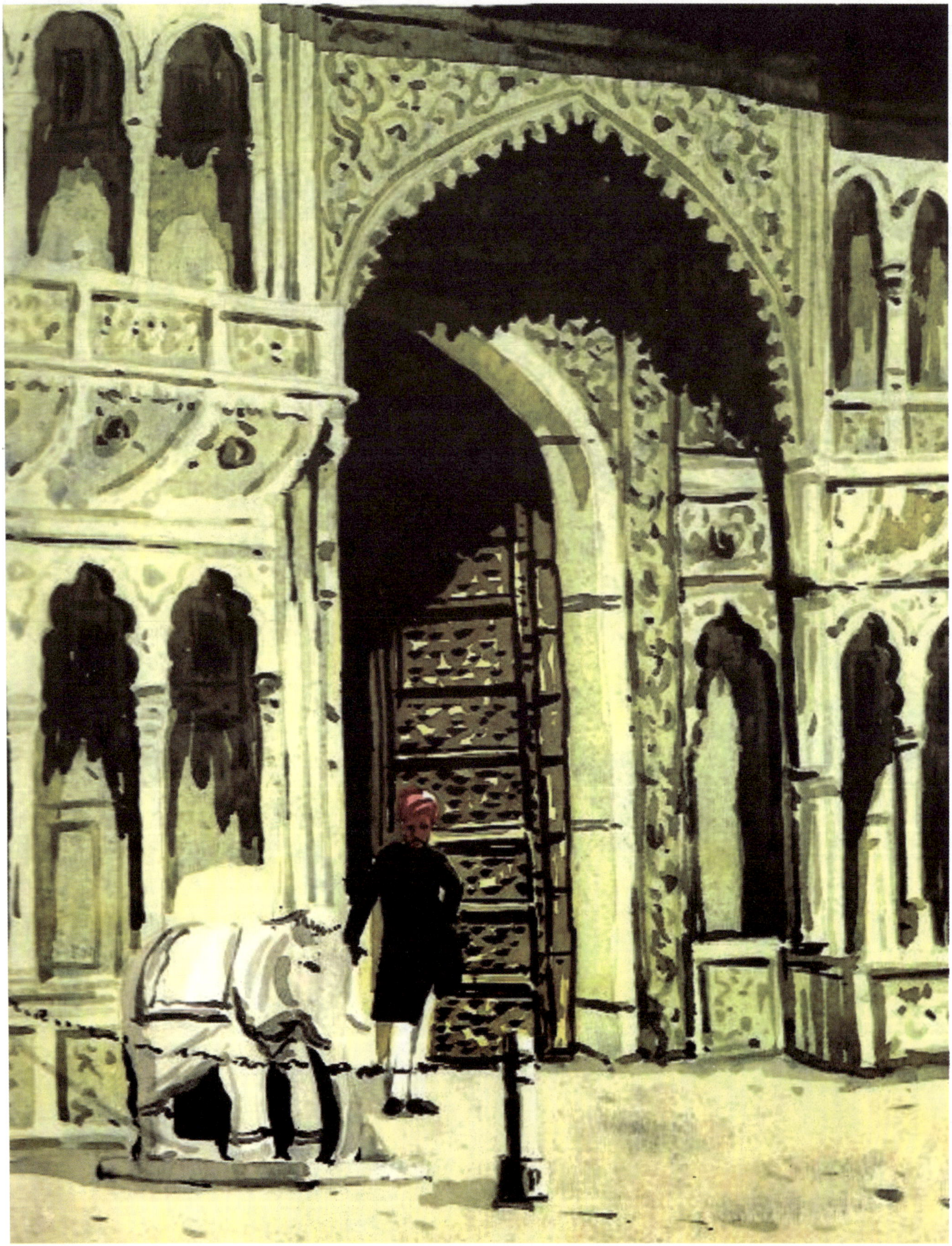

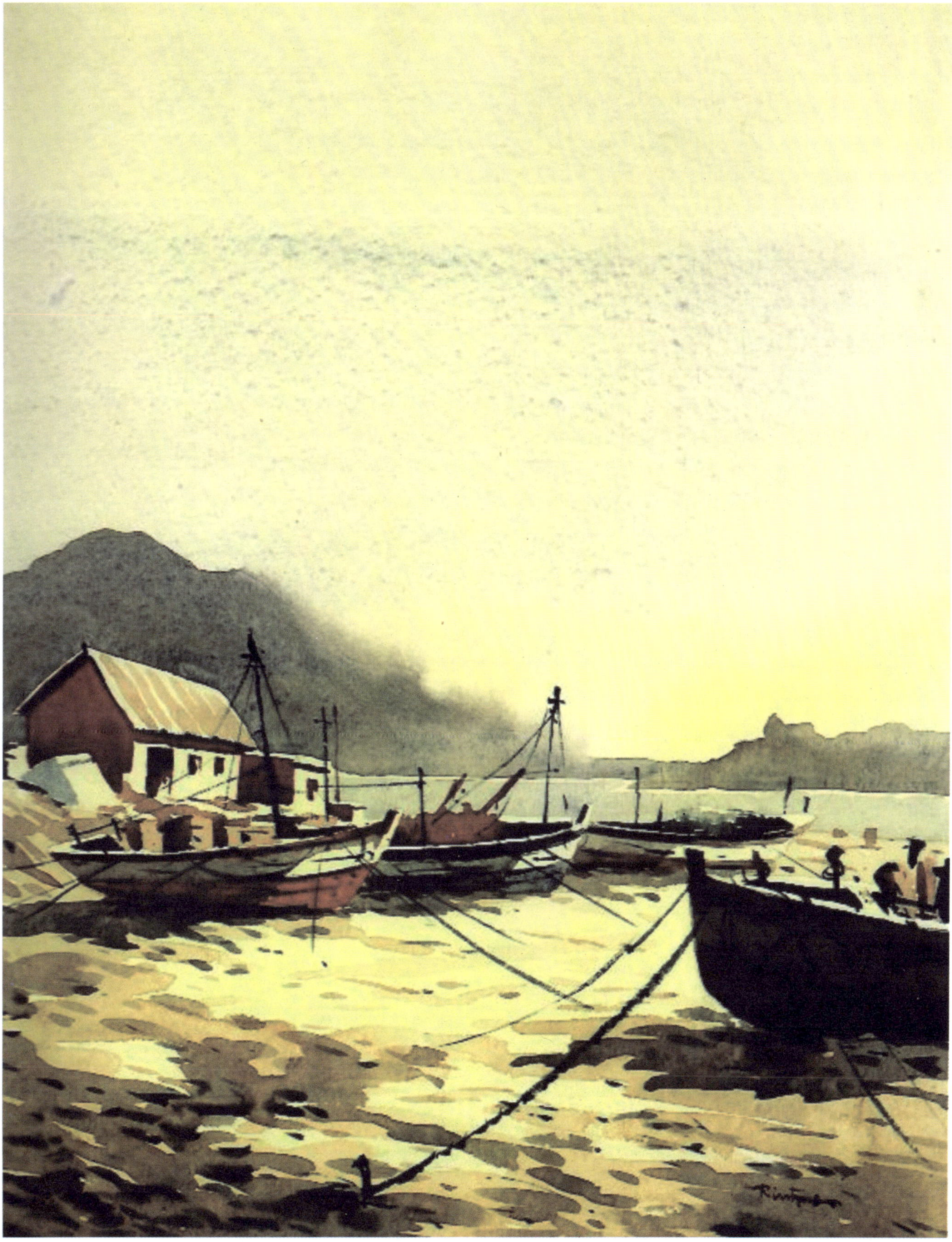

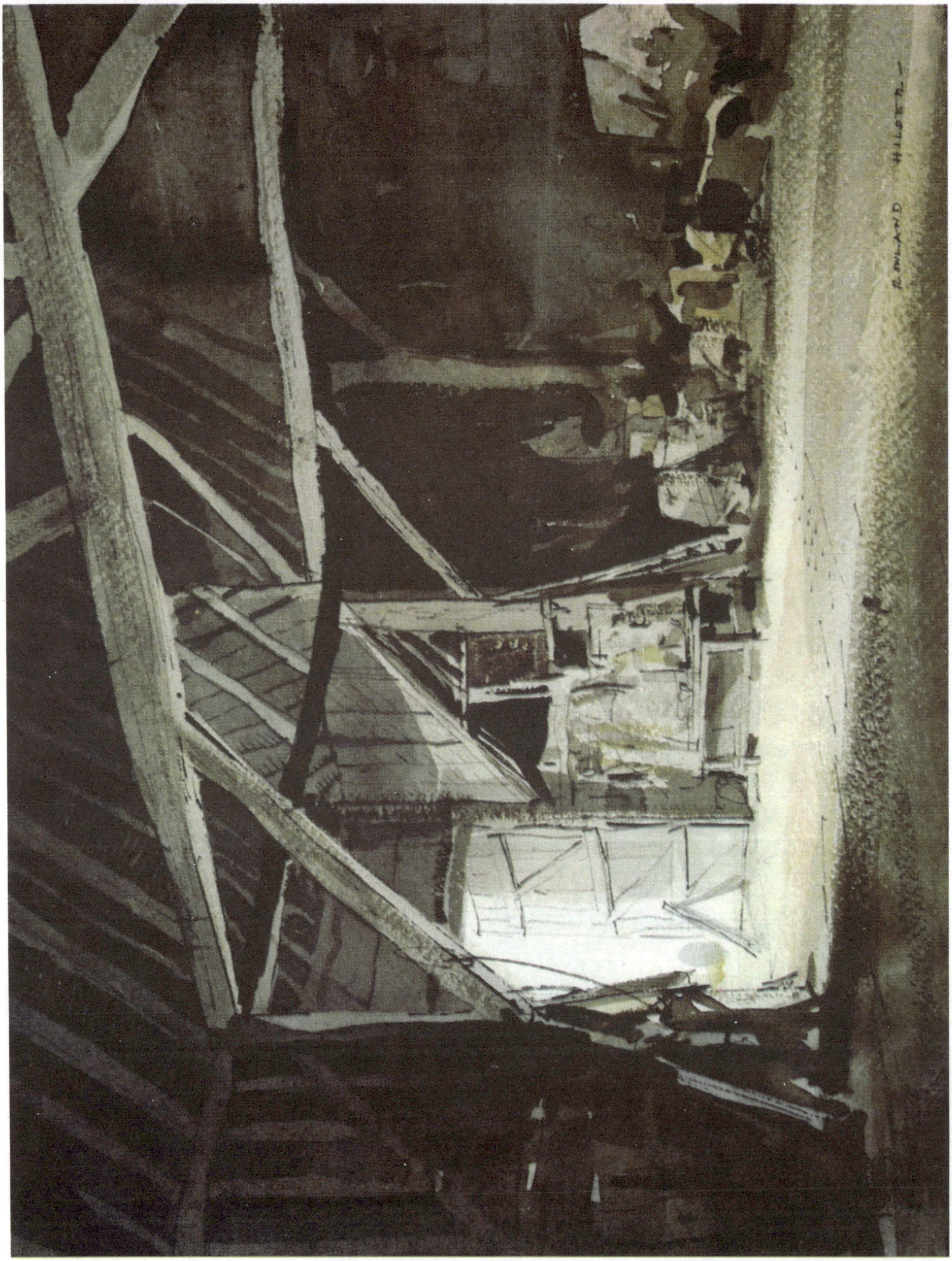
ROWLAND HILDER

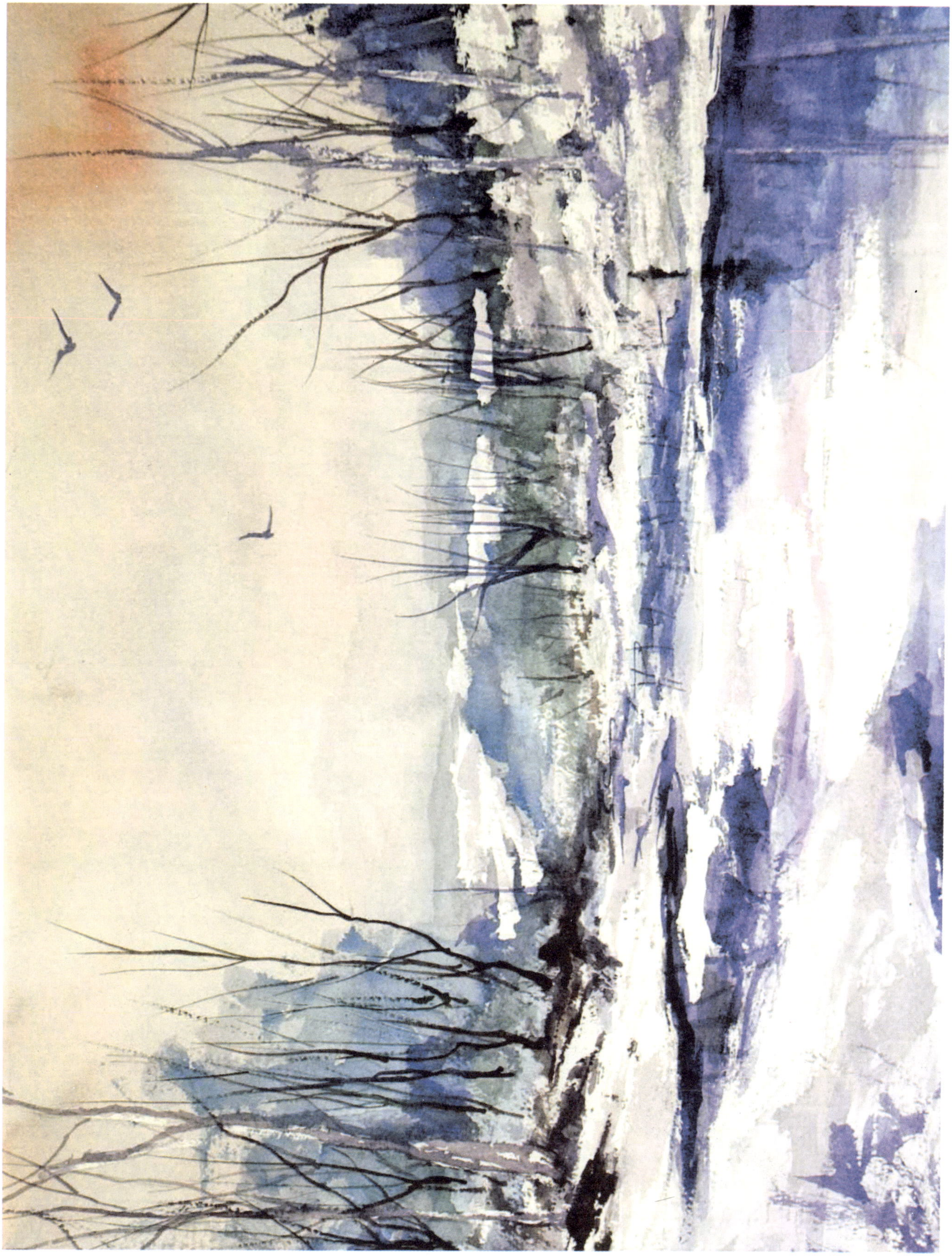

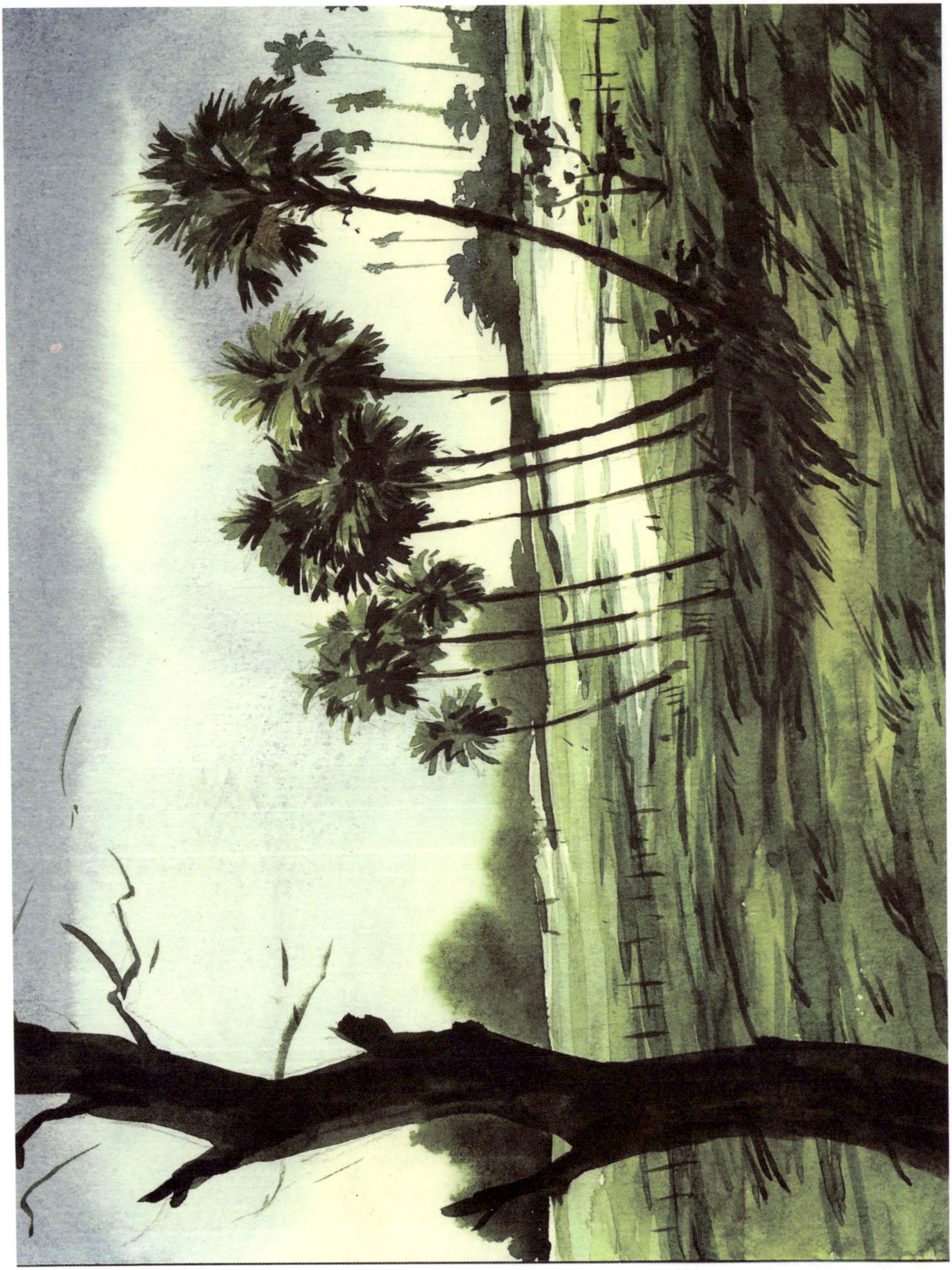

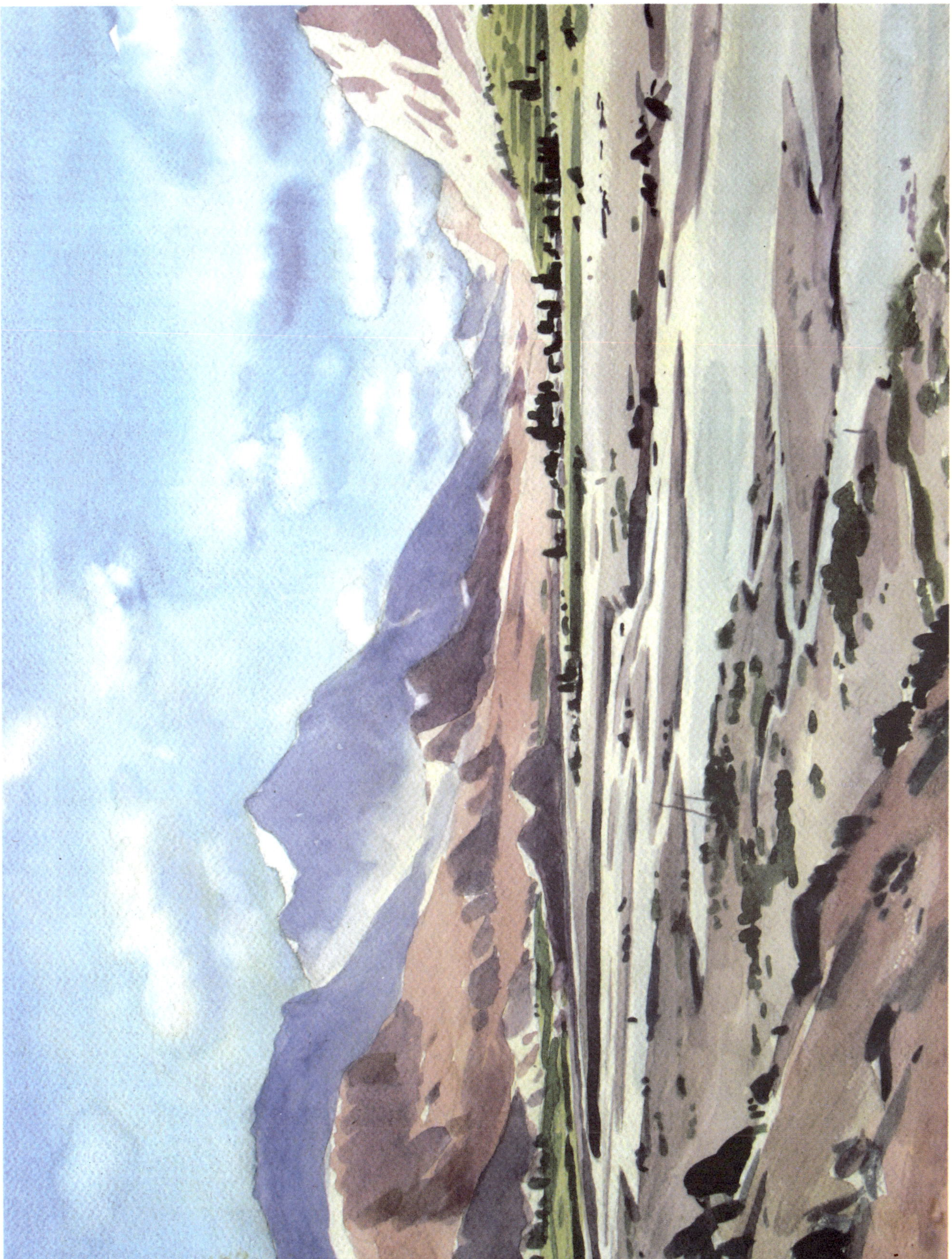

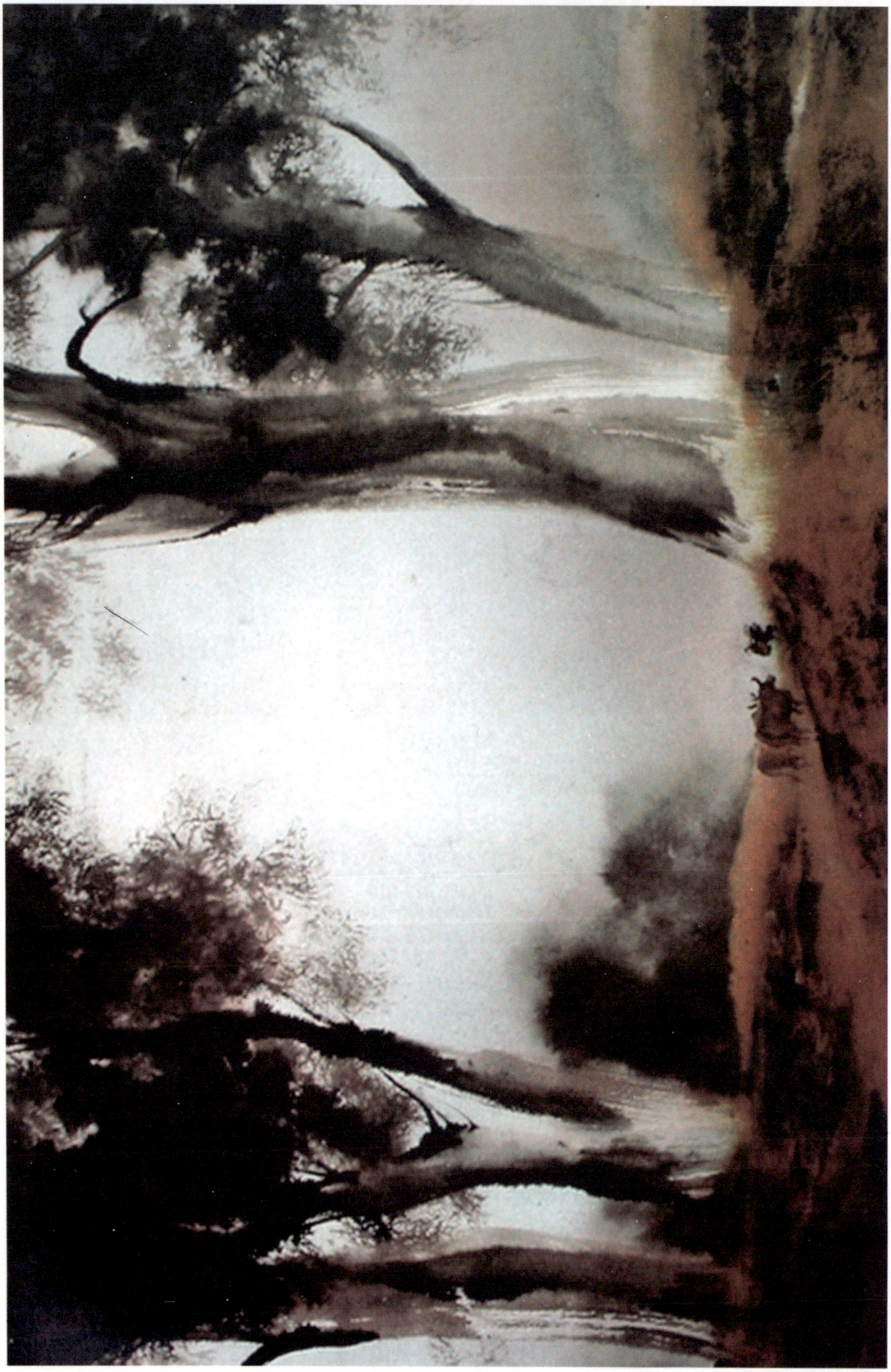

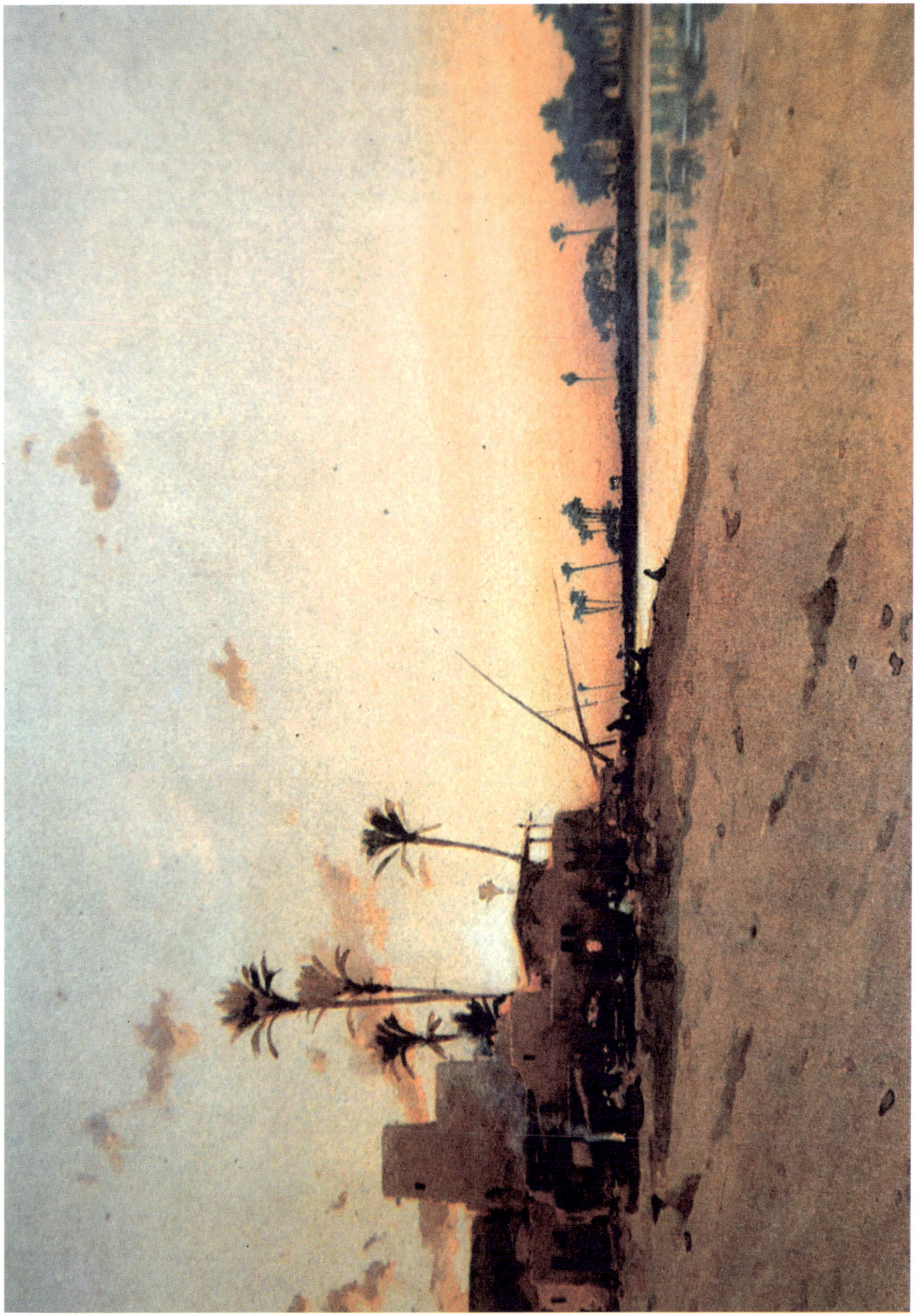

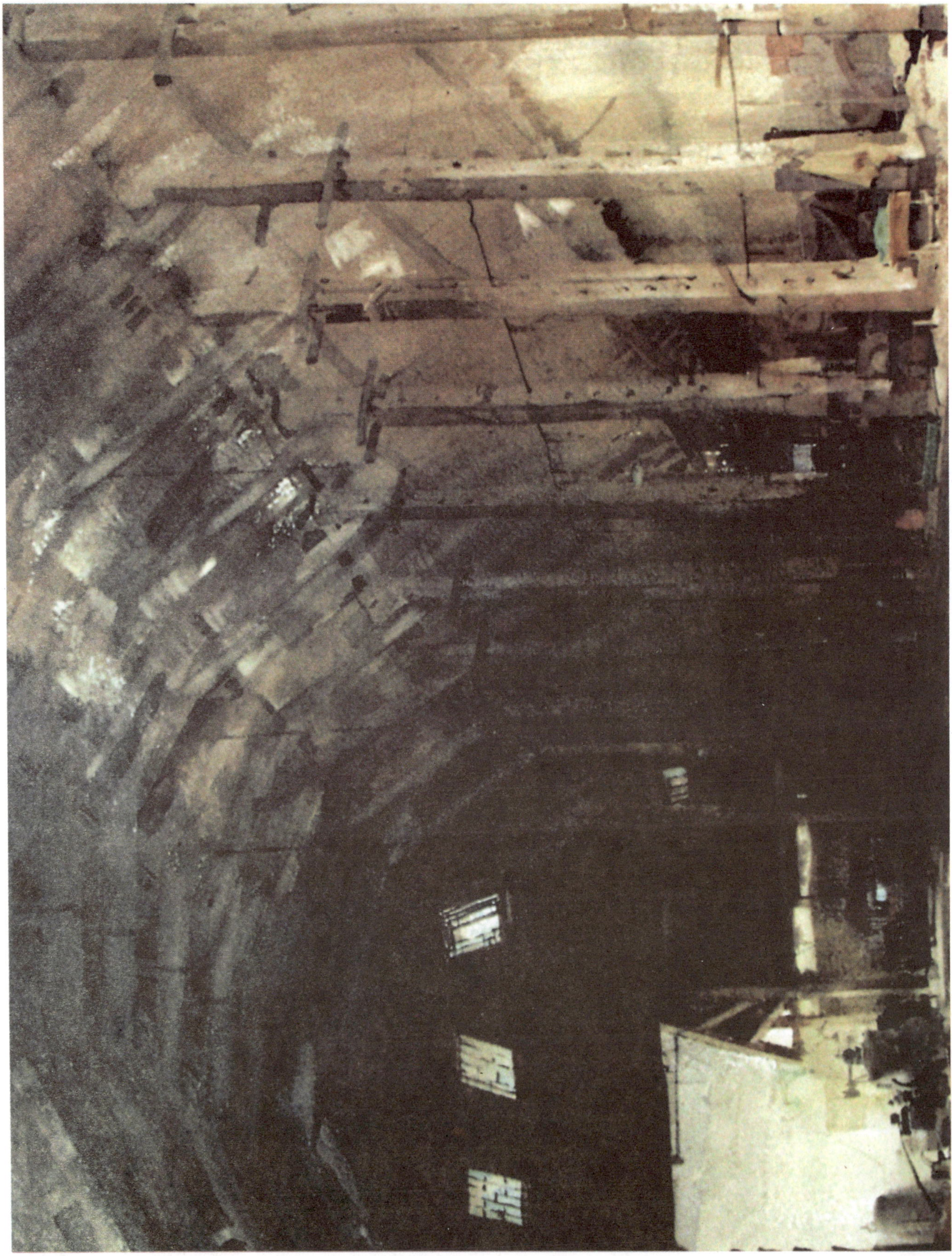

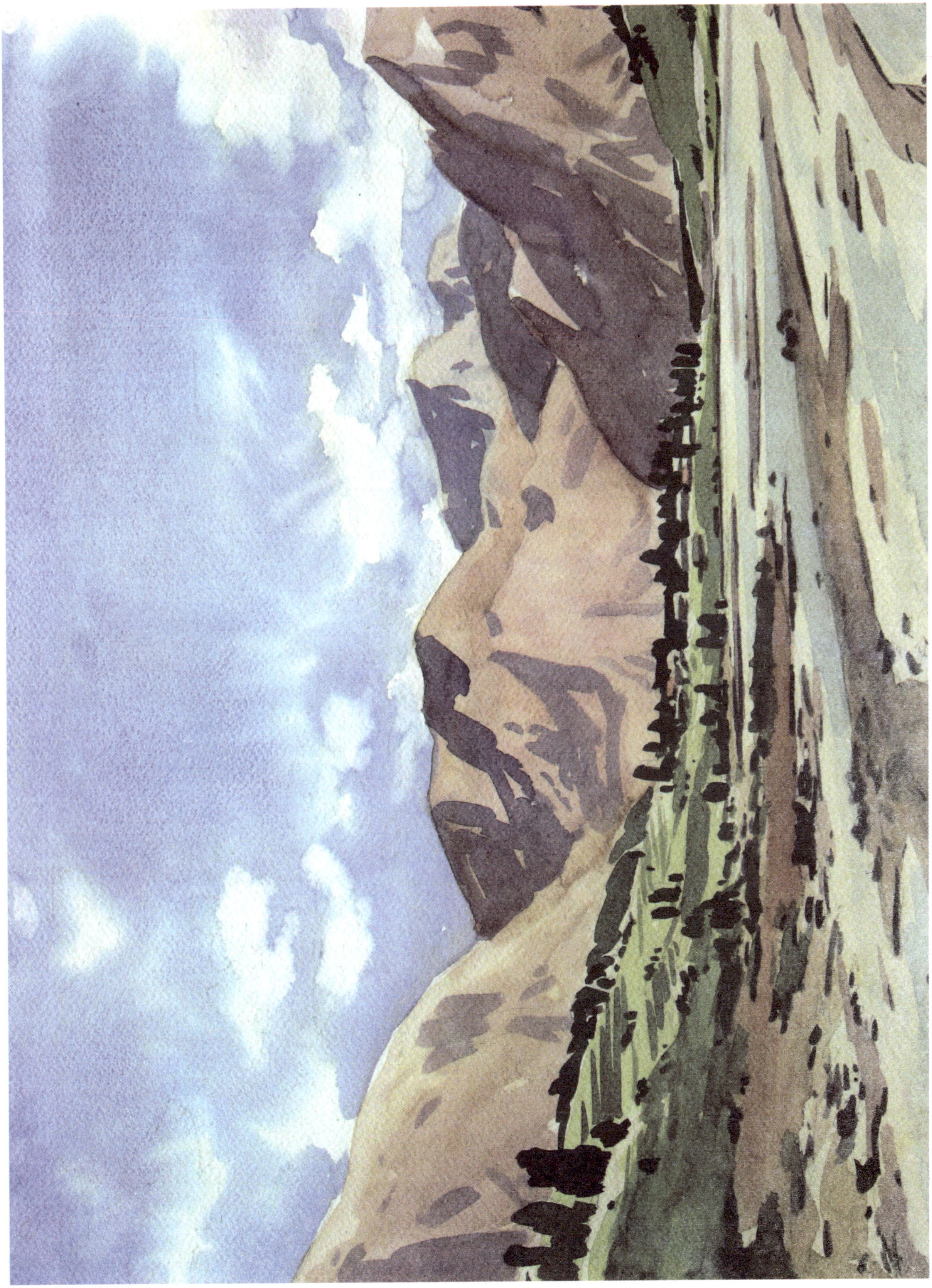

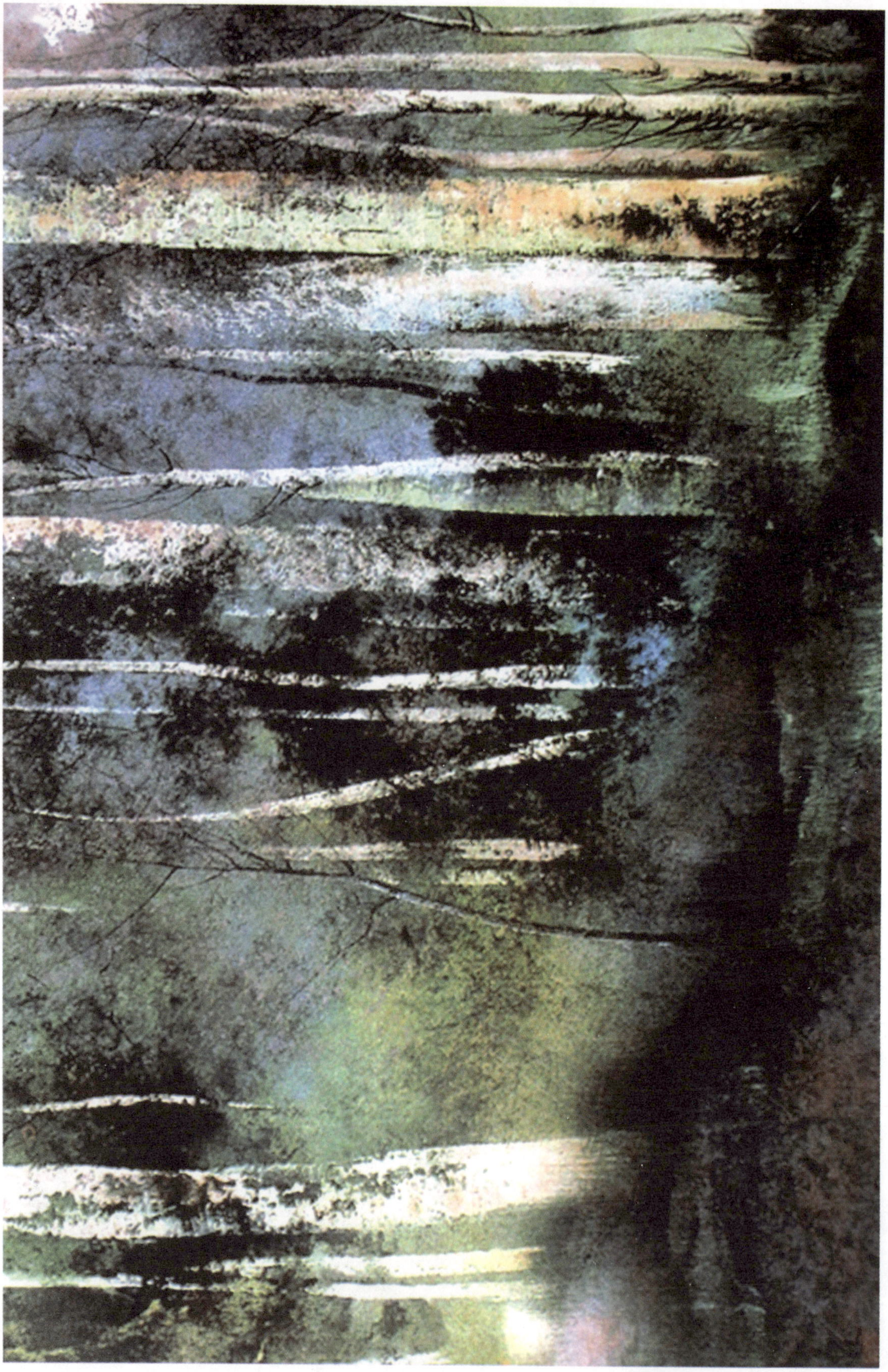

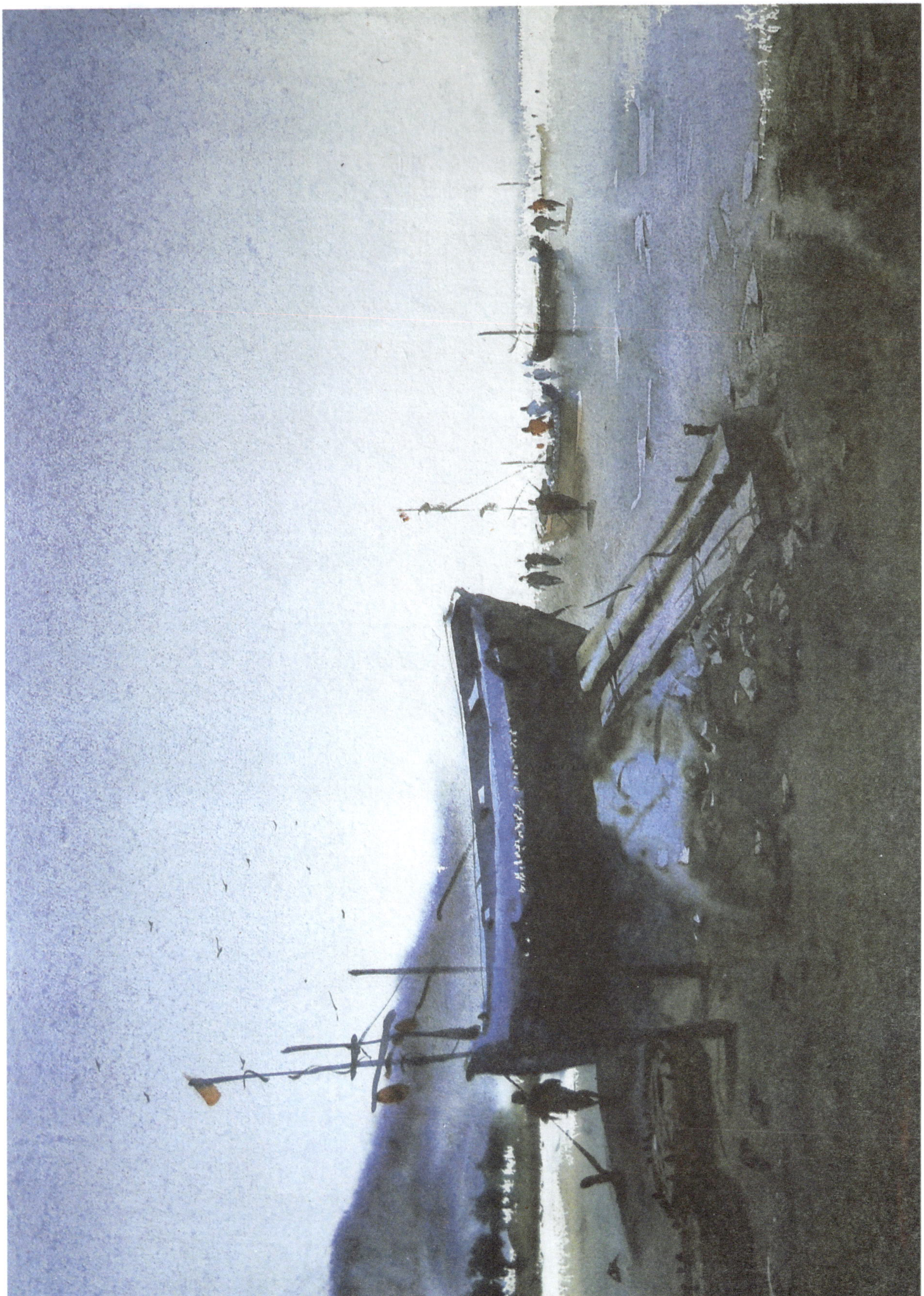

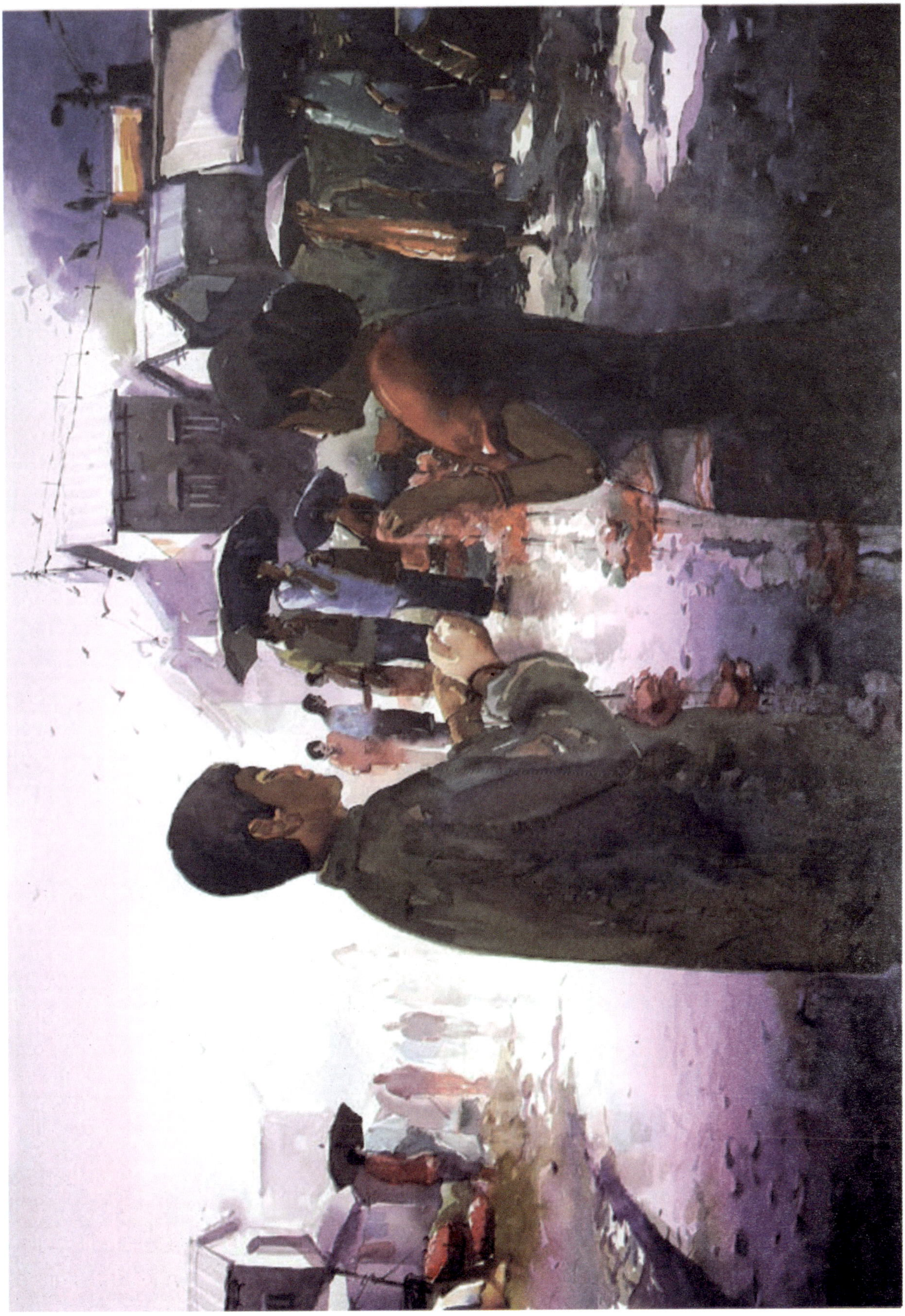

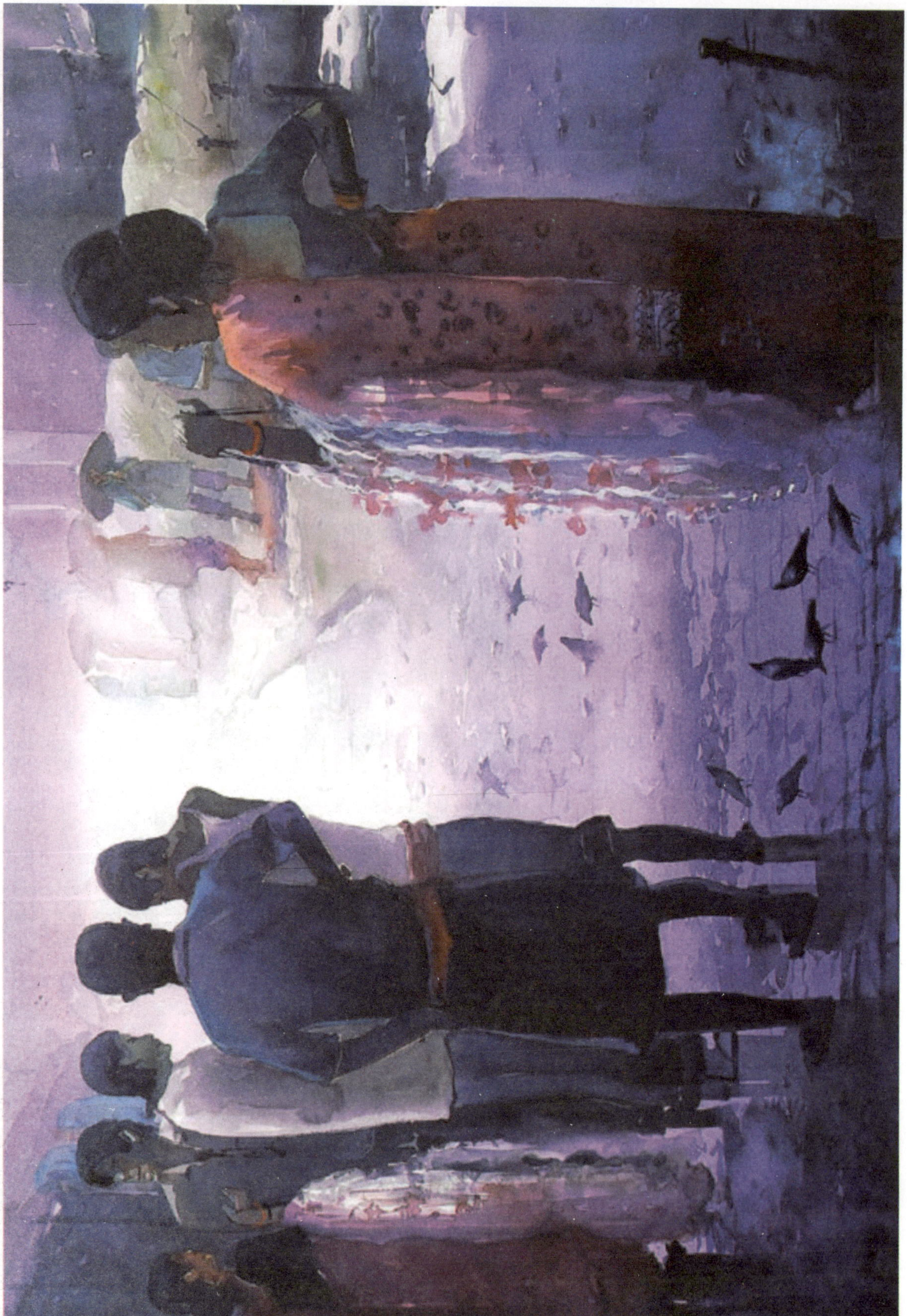